Stabilization Programs Implemented Under the Supervision of IMF

An Analysis of the Turkish Case

Stabilization Programs Implemented Under the Supervision of IMF

An Analysis of the Turkish Case

Professor Sadi Uzunoğlu

ATHENA PRESS
LONDON

CONTENTS

Introduction   vii

I Reasons for the 2000 stabilization program
and trends in the Turkish and world economies
at the beginning of the program   27

    1.1 *Changes in the Turkish economy and
political structure*   30

    1.2 *Asian crisis and trends in the world economy and
political structure*   37

II An analysis of the IMF program of 2000:
why and how was it implemented?   41

    2.1 *Targets of the 2000 stabilization program and
outline of the policies to be implemented*   41

    2.2 *Why did the program prove unsuccessful?*   54

III Transition to a stronger economy program
adopted after the February 2001 crisis and
assessment of its results   83

    3.1 *Main features of the transition to a stronger
economy program*   83

    3.2 *End of the transition to a stronger economy program,
September 11 attacks, and a new three-year program
in 2002*   100

    3.3 *Overview of the targets, strategies, and policies in
the letter of intent submitted to the IMF at the
beginning of 2002*   103

3.4 *Did the program of 2002 targeted to be implemented
for three years prove successful?* 119

IV Will the current program and the new program
of 2005 with the IMF prove successful?
How and under which conditions? 123

4.1 *Turkey should avoid any kind of "stress" that
would involve political risks and achieve a wide
range consensus throughout society* 125

4.2 *Economic relations with the neighboring countries
should be improved, expanding joint interests.
The position and function of Turkey in GMEP
(Greater Middle East Project) should not create
any risk* 128

4.3 *Structural Problems* 134

4.4 *Structural reforms must be implemented for a
sustainable growth* 145

4.5 *Every year a sizeable (US $7–8 billion) amount
of foreign direct investment must be attracted to
the country. And the incoming capital must not
only meet domestic demand but also contribute
to exports and employment* 147

4.6 *Turkish lira must not be overvalued* 148

4.7 *Long-term domestic and foreign debts
must be found and costs must be decreased* 161

4.8 *There must be a net positive primary surplus in
a stable growing economy without restricting
social needs* 162

Conclusion 171

References 190

INTRODUCTION

During a period of thirty years, Turkey has experienced high and chronic inflation along with an unstable growth. Among the reasons for this trend that has prevailed since the early 1970s, a number of domestic and foreign factors, and shock can be cited: the Cyprus crisis and subsequent embargo policy of the USA against Turkey, Turkey's industrial structure being not ready for competition, the weight of the agricultural sector in the economy and problems with its transformation, Turkey's demographic structure, the liberalization implementations after 1980 lacking a proper infrastructure, the inflationary impacts of the infrastructure investments supported by foreign finances, the public sector deficits and financing schemes, populist policies, the insistence on financing the current account deficit with hot money, and so on.

At the end of 1999, Turkey signed a Stand-By Arrangement with the IMF with the aim to solve her chronic problems of budget deficit and high inflation, and to decrease the ratio of the public sector debt to the national income below 60 percent (an EU criterion). Even though there was substantial international support for the program at the beginning, the crisis which had begun in November 2000 resulted in a devaluation in February 2001. This meant the end of the so-called peg to the foreign currency system. After the February devaluation, the floating foreign currency regime was adopted. The IMF-supported Transition to a Stronger Economy Program focused on the liquidity problem with an aim to stabilize the foreign currency and interest rates. However, a new three-year Stand-by Arrangement was signed at the beginning of 2002 due to the September 11 attacks and changing international conjuncture. The current program which is projected to last till the first months of 2005 began in February 2002. While the program is found successful by "certain parts of society", the IMF has announced by all means that things are going well as projected, considering their efforts in this success (a support of US $23 billion).

However, in mid-2004 we must acknowledge the existence of a serious confusion in public opinion caused by the economic data and related assessments. Yet, the discussion among the economy administrators in August implies that there are some troubles. If everything is going well, what is the reason for this panic that they feel? Why has the IMF staff been invited to Turkey to sign a new agreement for 2005 under the pretext of "technical infrastructure studies"? Why do the fiscal sector "experts" state that a new three-year agreement with the IMF is indispensable? Why do the authorities from the business world announce that "the interest rates will decrease by at least 4 points if we sign an agreement with the IMF"?

In the first half of 2004, the current account deficit has reached US $10 billion. The Minister of State responsible for the economy declares that a new program with social concerns has been prepared; but why does he not accept in public that, due to the negative effects on the budget of the measures to reduce the foreign trade and current account deficits, the implementations to be adopted as a result of the eighth Review of 2004 and the new program will constitute the most serious threat to a program with social concerns? Why does he not discuss publicly that they have to increase the prices of the public sector products and services (above all, those of energy) to meet the primary surplus target, and that this implementation is in contradiction with the inflation target?

If the vulnerable structure frequently referred to by the IMF continues, if Turkey is the second country having the highest real interest burden with Brazil, if Turkey is trying to agree with the IMF immediately, and if she needs a new three-year agreement, why is the success or failure of the current program in the economy not opened to discussion? Why are the IMF support and the EU negotiations always on the agenda, and why is the EU used as a peg? Why is the lack of foreign direct investment in Turkey considered a result of the ambiguous process of the EU negotiations? Why does Turkey prefer an expectation management instead of solving her problems? All these questions are occupying and will continue to occupy the economic agenda.

This study analyzes the IMF-supported programs implemented in Turkey since 2000, and explores the answer to this question: Will the current program and the subsequent three-year program under the supervision of the IMF prove successful, and what are the conditions for a successful program?

*

At the beginning of the study, there is a chronology consisting of the economic and political trends in Turkey and the world economy, and of the relations between the IMF and Turkey. The chronology ends with the new program of end-1999.

Chapter I provides an overview of the reasons for the 2000 stabilization program in the light of the economic and political trends in Turkey and the world economy. In the section which provides the contexts of the Asian crisis, the subsequent world conjuncture, and Turkey's significance after this process, the basic problems and dilemmas of the Turkish economy are discussed.

Chapter II presents the outlines of the IMF program with the peg system in 2000. The reasons for the failure of the program are discussed as well. This will enable us to discover that the reasons behind the failure of the 2000 program cannot be simply explained as the dispute between Turkish Prime Minister Bülent Ecevit and President Ahmet Necdet Sezer during the meeting of the National Security Council that ignited the 2001 crisis. Rather, there were macroeconomic inequilibria, a vulnerability in the fiscal system, hesitations and uncertainties in implementing the structural reforms, which all led to a compulsory devaluation.

The Transition to a Stronger Economy Program which was implemented after the February 2001 devaluation, the subsequent three-year program which began in February 2002, and the problems with the implementation of these two programs will be the focus of Chapter III. In addition, it provides the grounds for the new program to be implemented in 2005 under the supervision of the IMF.

Chapter IV deals with the necessary conditions for the success of the new three-year program to be implemented in 2005 after the program of 2002. The study ends with the conclusion.

*

I am gratefully indebted to Uğur Civelek for providing critical comments.

I would also like to thank Sermin Güngör, Serkan Yürük, Şafak Korkut, Abdurrrahman Erzaim, my professor Veysi Seviğ and Erdoğan Çankaya.

I would like to mention that errors and omissions, if any, in this study are exclusively mine. I would like to highlight that this study is written in plain language to address a readership that may not be familiar with economic theories and concepts.

Sadi Uzunoğlu
July 2004

CHRONOLOGY: TRENDS IN TURKISH AND THE WORLD ECONOMY, AND AGREEMENTS WITH THE IMF

Economic and Political Developments in Turkey	IMF Chronology	Agreements between Turkey and the IMF	Trends in the World
1946 First multiparty elections. Turkish Lira is devalued in accordance with September 7 decisions.	**July 1944** IMF and World Bank Articles of Agreement are formulated at the International Monetary and Financial Conference, Bretton Woods, New Hampshire, USA. **December 1945** Articles of Agreement enter into force upon signature by 29 governments. **May 1946** Twelve Executive Directors hold inaugural meeting in Washington DC, USA. **September–October 1946** First Annual Meetings of Boards of Governors of IMF and World Bank.	**September 1946** Application for membership to IMF: First devaluation by Republican People's Party (CHP) government headed by Recep Peker; rate 53.6 percent.	**1944** Bretton Woods agreements creating the World Bank & the International Monetary Fund. **1945** End of the World War II. **March 1947** The Truman Doctrine. **June 1947** The Marshall Plan (Economic Cooperation Act) for European reconstruction. **April 4, 1949** Establishment of NATO.

Economic and Political Developments in Turkey	IMF Chronology	Agreements between Turkey and the IMF	Trends in the World
	March 1947 IMF begins operations. **May 1947** First drawing from IMF (by France).	**April 1947** Full membership of Turkey. First quota: US $43 million.	
1950–59 Efforts to get involved in international relations. **May 14, 1950** General Elections: Democratic Party (DP) in power. **September 20, 1951** Turkey's membership of NATO. **1954** General Elections: DP government won once more.	**August 1952** Germany and Japan become members. **October 1952** Executive Board approves proposals for standardized Stand-By Arrangements.	**August 1958** Increasing pressure from IMF. Additional tax of TL 6.22 per dollar is imposed on foreign currency purchase. A devaluation of 69 percent is realized in practice.	**1950** Korean War, rapid growth of the USA economy.

Economic and Political Developments in Turkey	IMF Chronology	Agreements between Turkey and the IMF	Trends in the World
1957 General Elections: DP government remained in power despite its decreasing votes. **1958** For the first time in Cyprus, British army has recourse to force against Turkish people.			**March 1957** European Economic Community (EEC) created via the Treaty of Rome.
1960–1970 Frequent negotiations with IMF.		**1960** 1 US $ is equal to TL 9.	**1960** Establishment of London Gold Fund due to rush of speculators to gold.
1960 Military coup d'état.		**January 1, 1961** First Stand-by arrangement with IMF: SDR 21.5 million is agreed on. SDR 16.5 million is drawn.	
July 1961 A new constitution is in force.		**March 30, 1962** Stand-by arrangement: SDR 31 million is agreed on. SDR 15 million is drawn.	

Economic and Political Developments in Turkey	IMF Chronology	Agreements between Turkey and the IMF	Trends in the World
October 1961 General Elections: Government coalition of Republican People's Party (CHP) and Justice Party (AP). **September 1963** Conclusion of "Ankara Agreement", the Association Agreement between Turkey and EMU.	**January 1962** Executive Board adopts terms and conditions of General Arrangements to Borrow (GAB). **February 1963** Compensatory Financing Facility is created.	**March 15, 1963** Stand-by arrangement: SDR 21.5 million is agreed on. SDR 21.5 million is drawn. **February 15, 1964** Stand-by arrangement: SDR 21.5 million is agreed on. SDR 19 million is drawn. **February 1, 1965** Stand-by arrangement: SDR 21.5 million is agreed on. Nothing is drawn.	**Second half of the 1960s** US $ is under pressure in international financial markets.
October1965 General Elections: AP in power, Demirel is prime minister for the first time.		**February 1, 1966** Stand-by arrangement: SDR 21 million is agreed on. SDR 21.5 million is drawn.	

Economic and Political Developments in Turkey	IMF Chronology	Agreements between Turkey and the IMF	Trends in the World
1967 Famous "triumvira" are in power; Özal is undersecretary of State Planning Agency, Talu president of Central Bank, Cantürk secretary general of Treasury.	**September 1967** Board of Governors approves plan to establish special drawing rights (SDRs).	**February 15, 1967** Stand-by arrangement: SDR 21 million is agreed on. SDR 27 million is drawn. **April 1, 1968** Stand-by arrangement: SDR 27 million is agreed on. SDR 27 million is drawn.	**November 1967** Devaluation of Sterling. **1968** Termination of Gold Fund.
1967 Implementation of foreign currency indexed deposit.	**June 1969** Buffer Stock Financing Facility is established. **1970** First allocation of SDRs.	**July 1, 1969** Stand-by arrangement: SDR 27 million is agreed on. SDR 10 million drawn. **August 1970** Devaluation of TL by 40 percent. **August 17, 1970** Stand-by arrangement: SDR 90 million is agreed on. SDR 90 million is drawn.	**August 1969** Devaluation of French franc.

Economic and Political Developments in Turkey	IMF Chronology	Agreements between Turkey and the IMF	Trends in the World
1970–80 A period characterized by political instability and coalitions, rapid social changes and polarization, industrialization policies based on import substitution and planned economy, foreign debt and energy crisis.			
1971 Military Note and Erim Government.	**August 1971** United States informs IMF it will no longer freely buy and sell gold to settle international transactions. **December 1971** Smithsonian Agreement. **July 1972** Board of Governors adopts resolution establishing a Committee on Reform of the International Monetary System, known as the Committee of 20.	**1970–74** Cold relations with IMF due to political uncertainty in Turkey.	**December 1971** USA ended gold standard, devalued dollar by 9 percent, currency floats, establishment of wider margins according to Smithsonian Agreement. **March 1972** Adoption of "serpent in the tunnel" implementation by EEC countries.

Economic and Political Developments in Turkey	IMF Chronology	Agreements between Turkey and the IMF	Trends in the World
October 1973 General Elections: Coalition period. **January-September 1974** CHP-MSP Government. **July-August 1974** Cyprus Crisis and USA Embargo. **March 1975** First National Front Coalition Government.	**September 1974** IMF sets up Extended Fund Facility. **August 1975** Executive Board establishes a Subsidy Account, funded by contributions, to assist the most seriously affected members using the oil facility.	**1974** Revaluation: appreciation of TL against dollar by 11 percent.	**1973** OPEC Oil Crisis **March 1973** Demolition of Bretton Woods system. Transition to joint floats for currencies. **1974–75** Stagflation in economic stagnation.
1977 General Elections: Second National Front Coalition Government.	**May 1976** Executive Board establishes a Trust Fund. **August 1977** Executive Board establishes Supplementary Financing Facility.	**April 1975–June 1977** As a result of eight mini devaluations dollar exchange rate increased from TL 13.7 to TL 17.5 in September 1977 by 10 percent devaluation.	**1976** Jamaica meeting and introduction of SDR system. **1977–78** Foreign debt crises in developing countries.

Economic and Political Developments in Turkey	IMF Chronology	Agreements between Turkey and the IMF	Trends in the World
January 1978 CHP in power: Ecevit is prime minister for the second time. **August 1978** Removal of USA military embargo.	**September 1978** Interim Committee approves 50 percent quota increase which raises IMF general resources to SDR 58.6 billion.	**February 1978** 30 percent devaluation. **April 24, 1978** Stand-by arrangement: SDR 300 million is agreed on. SDR 90 million is drawn. **December 1978** Negotiations cut off. Turkey tries to find new sources till March 1979.	**February 1979** Islam Revolution in Iran and the second oil crisis. **March 1979** European Monetary system created to keep exchange rates stable. **December 1979** Occupation of Afghanistan by USSR.
October 1979 AP minority government in power.	**February 1979** Supplementary Financing Facility enters into force.	**July 19, 1979** Stand-by arrangement: SDR 250 million is agreed on. SDR 230 million is drawn.	
January 24, 1980 January 24 Decisions: First indications of the transition to liberal economy. **July 1980** Interest rates are liberalized.	**December 1980** Aggregate quotas are raised to SDR 60 billion.	**April 1980** Transition to frequent exchange rate adjustment regime, devaluations will not exceed 5 percent.	

Economic and Political Developments in Turkey	IMF Chronology	Agreements between Turkey and the IMF	Trends in the World
September 12, 1980 Military coup d'état, democracy is suspended. Özal in government.		**June 18, 1980** Stand-by arrangement: SDR 1,250 million is agreed on. SDR 1,250 million is drawn.	
1980–89 Years with Özal: Liberalization in economy and developments in foreign trade as a result of five Structural Adjustment Programs with the World Bank.			
	1981 IMF begins to use simplified basket of five currencies to determine daily valuation of SDR.	**1981** End of multiple exchange rate system, transition to crawling exchange rate regime: Rates to be announced on daily basis.	
June 1982 Banker crisis, resignation of Özal. **November 1982** New constitution is in power.	**August 1982** IMF supports major adjustment programs in Mexico and several other countries facing severe debt-servicing difficulties.	**April 4, 1983** Stand-by arrangement: SDR 225 million is agreed on. SDR 112.5 million is drawn.	**1981–87** Inflation fighting and inertia in developed countries.

Economic and Political Developments in Turkey	IMF Chronology	Agreements between Turkey and the IMF	Trends in the World
December 1982 Interest rates are again under the control of the Central Bank. **November 1983** General Elections: ANAP in power, Özal is prime minister.	**November 1983** Increases in quotas.	**June 24, 1983** Last Stand-by arrangement before 1995: SDR 225 million is agreed on. SDR 52.25 million is drawn.	**1982–84** Foreign exchange crises in developing countries, Latin America moratorium.
April 1987 Turkey applies for full membership to EMU. **September 1987** Referendum on lifting of political bans, banned politicians return to politics. **November 1987** General Elections: ANAP government in power again.	**March 1986** IMF establishes Structural Adjustment Facility (SAF). **December 1987** IMF establishes Enhanced Structural Adjustment Facility (ESAF).		**October 1987** Black Monday: New York Stock Market crash. Crises in developed countries. Market formation and deregulation speeded up.

Economic and Political Developments in Turkey	IMF Chronology	Agreements between Turkey and the IMF	Trends in the World
November 1988 Interest rates are liberalized.	**August 1988** IMF Executive Board establishes Compensatory and Contingency Financing Facility.	**Years without IMF** Turkey easily finds foreign finances in international markets.	
August 1989 With Decree no.32 of parliament, liberalization in foreign exchange regime and capital movements. **September 1989** Referendum on constitution change. **November 1989** Özal is president.			**1989** Cold War won by USA and its allies, disintegration of socialist block, liberal democracy and market economy being appreciated.
1990–2000 Political and social instability and stagnation, economic crises.			

Economic and Political Developments in Turkey	IMF Chronology	Agreements between Turkey and the IMF	Trends in the World
June 1991 Elected by ANAP Congress, Mesut Yılmaz is prime minister. **October 1991** General Elections: DYP-SHP coalition. **March 1992** Terrorism is alarming, turmoil during Nevruz celebration.	**May 1990** Interim Committee agrees to 50 percent quota increase, to SDR 135.2 billion. **April-May 1992** Executive Board approves membership of countries of the former Soviet Union. **June 1992** IMF approves the membership of Russia.	**1990** TL's convertibility is approved by IMF, and Turkish Lira is accepted as foreign currency.	**1990–91** Persian Gulf War, declaration of new world order. **1991** Fall of USSR. **February 1992** Maastricht Treaty creating European Union (EU).
April-June 1993 Özal is dead, Demirel is president, Tansu Çiller prime minister.	**August 1992** IMF approves SDR 719 million Stand-by Arrangement for Russia. **May 1993** Kyrgyz Republic is first member to use STF.		

Economic and Political Developments in Turkey	IMF Chronology	Agreements between Turkey and the IMF	Trends in the World
January-February 1994 Economic crisis; TL depreciated by 60 percent in two months, treasury bond interest rates reach 400 percent. **April 5, 1994** Decisions and stabilization program. **1994** Current account trade deficit yields a surplus of US $2.6 billion, but growth rate is -6.1 percent.	**June 1994** IMF announces creation of three Deputy Managing Director posts.	**April 1994** TL is devalued by 30 percent. **July 1994** SDR 160.5 million is drawn from IMF; consolidated budget deficit is performance criterion. **July 8, 1994** 14 month-Stand-by arrangement SDR 590.2 million is agreed on. **November 1994** SDR 75 million is drawn; limitation on extra-budgetary borrowings to SEEs is performance criterion.	
March 1995 Introduction of the customs union with EU. **December 1995** General Elections: RP is the first party, but does not have single party majority.	**February 1995** Executive Board approves a Stand-By Arrangement of SDR 12.1 billion for Mexico.	**November 1995 and February 1996** Last two portions of SDR 75 million each cannot be drawn, because Turkey has fallen short of her budgetary and monetary performance criteria, an amount of SDR 460.5 million has been used.	**February 1995** Mexico Crisis and its expansion to Latin America with "Tequila effect".

Economic and Political Developments in Turkey	IMF Chronology	Agreements between Turkey and the IMF	Trends in the World
February 1996 ANAYOL coalition. **July 1996** REFAHYOL coalition: Alternately first prime minister is Erbakan, Çiller foreign affairs minister.	**March 1996** Executive Board approves an SDR 6.9 billion Extended Fund Facility for Russia, the largest EFF in IMF history.		
February 28, 1997 Political crisis following the meeting of National Security Council, secret note to government. **July 1997** ANASOL-D minority government.	**November 1997** Executive Board approves a Stand-By Arrangement of SDR 10 billion for Indonesia. **December 1997** Executive Board approves a Stand-By Arrangement of SDR 15.5 billion for Korea, the largest financial commitment in IMF history.	**April 1997** Usual annual negotiations with IMF. **October 1997** Evaluation of the economic developments in Turkey by IMF delegation.	**1997** Asian Crisis shaking the world, the biggest and widespread crisis after Bretton Woods.

Economic and Political Developments in Turkey	IMF Chronology	Agreements between Turkey and the IMF	Trends in the World
January 1998 With the transfer of Interbank to SDIF, the number of Fund banks is 3.	**December 1998** A Stand-By Arrangement of SDR 13 billion for Brazil.	**June 1998** Staff-Monitored Program put into effect.	**August 1998** Russian Crisis, a moratorium of 90 days is declared for foreign debts.
January 1999 DSP minority government. **April 1999** General Elections: DSP-MHP-ANAP Coalition. **August-November 1999** Marmara earthquake.	**July 1999** A Stand-By Arrangement of SDR 3.3 billion for Russia for a period of 17 months.	**October 1999** To compensate earthquake losses, an emergency support of SDR 361.5 million is provided to Turkey.	**October 1998** Russian Crisis spreads to Latin America, global recession risk.
December 1999 Five more banks are taken over, banking sector in trouble, the economy has contracted by 6 percent.		**December 1999** Based on the letter of intent within the framework of Turkey's disinflation program, the stand-by arrangement of SDR 2.9 billion is accepted. First portion is SDR 221.7 million. Foreign exchange rates are pre-determined for a period of 18 months.	**January 1999** Introduction of the Euro currency in 11 countries. **December 1999** The world preparing for the new Millennium, Y2K problem is the nightmare of IT sector.

CHAPTER I

Reasons for the 2000 stabilization program and trends in the Turkish and world economies at the beginning of the program

Turkey has been one of the countries experiencing chronic inflation since the early 1970s; she ended up being the country with the most permanent inflation. Like in other countries, chronic inflation imposed a heavy burden on the fiscal system, and caused an escape from the national currency. Savings depositors tended to purchase assets such as gold, foreign currency and/or real estate with the aim to protect their purchasing power, with the exception of those who had obligations such as tax payments. Thus, the national savings shifted to inefficient areas. Future expectations were indexed to a great extent to an enduring memory of inflation. The indexation led to a fluctuating inflation, stabilizing at around 30 percent at one time, and 50 percent at another, or rising to a higher plateau.

High public sector deficits and financing methods were the main causes of inflation. The inefficient use of resources and unproductivity due to inflation are the basic problems of the countries with chronic inflation. Turkish economy operated for a long period of time within an unproductive and inefficient structure. Budget deficit led to high interest rates which further reinforced the imbalance, and the financial liberalization process which began in 1989 caused the economy to face the risk of interest and foreign exchange rates.

Enduring instability of prices in the Turkish economy for long years increased the uncertainty, worsening the inequality of incomes. All these factors, along with the unproductivity and wastage of resources, resulted in an unstable growth. The deterioration in the investment-savings balance and high public

Graph 1. Turkey's Adventure of Inflation (WPI, CPI)

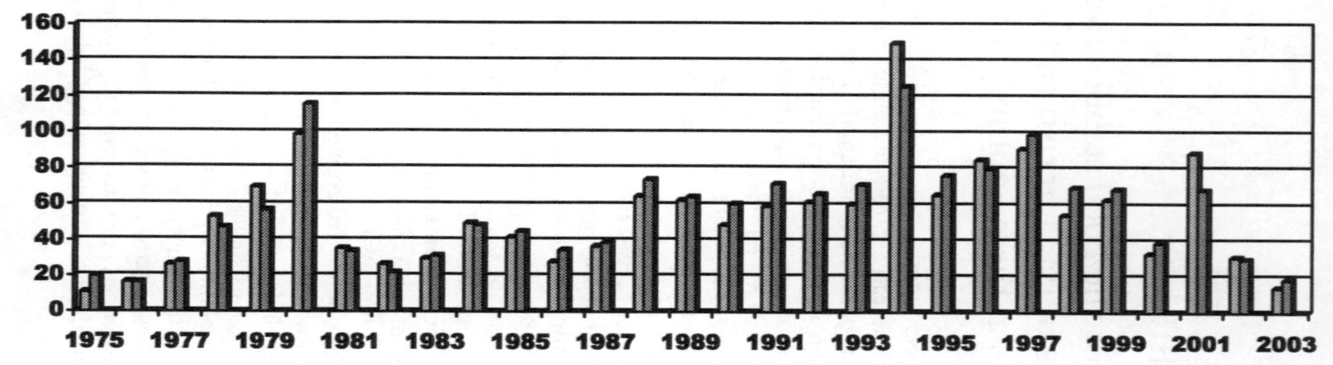

SOURCE: SIS (STATE INSTITUTE OF STATISTICS)

Graph 2. Unstable Growth Process in Turkey (%)

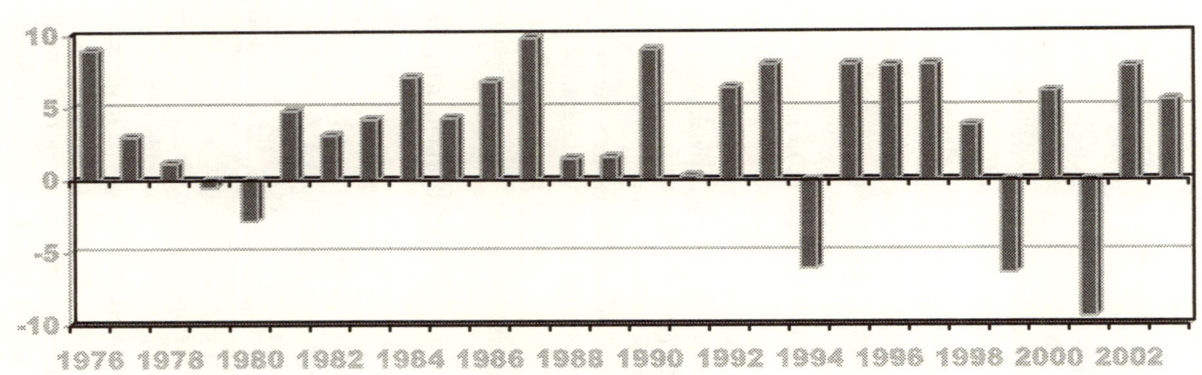

SOURCE: SIS

sector deficit in the Turkish economy naturally led to a foreign currency imbalance. Balances were further disturbed, and interest rates tended to increase more at the times when the Turkish economy had difficulties in reducing its foreign currency deficit. Whenever the Turkish economy had difficulties in finding external sources, the outcome was the same because it was impossible to raise the savings to a level high enough to close the public sector deficit.

This vicious circle had to be broken. High inflation and unstable growth were increasing the uncertainty; the increasing public sector deficit along with the sustainability of debt were the main problems. Turkey was at the end of the road. Since mid-1997 the economy administration was aware that something had to be done, and began to express it. In mid-1998 Turkey agreed with the IMF on a Staff-Monitored Program. However, the Program was interrupted by the April 1999 elections. Yet there was no turning back, and a Stand-By Arrangement was signed with the IMF at the end of 1999.

In order to better understand the new process under the supervision of the IMF, and to explore the factors leading to a failure in the disinflation program that began at the beginning of 2000, it is necessary to make an overview of the developments both in Turkey and abroad.

1.1 Changes in the Turkish economy and political structure

After the 1994 crisis, Turkey was in a net foreign debt repayer position. This position brought along a reliance on "hot money". As it would be observed in the following years, policies were dependent upon the inflow of hot money, and Turkey's future was indexed to the hot money inflow.

In 1996 the Customs Union between Turkey and the EU came into effect, and the foreign trade deficit began to widen. However, in order to prevent uneasiness in the markets due to the high external deficit, the foreign suitcase trade was included in the accounts. The economy was on a trend of growth, and Turkey was not in a difficult position as regards finding foreign sources.

Despite the political uncertainty, interest rates fell gradually as a result of growth and foreign sources. This was the conjuncture in 1997. The coalition government of the Welfare Party and True Path Party was in power. The economy administration of the time made an amendment in the borrowing strategy; they began with tax collection; they imposed a withholding tax for the first time on bonds; and most significantly, they borrowed in foreign currency instead of Turkish Lira. This was an attempt to decrease the debt cost. In the meantime, a serious political uncertainty was prevailing, which had a negative effect on the new source package attempts including the unpaid non-quota import attempts. The domestic debts were redeemed with the foreign currency borrowings and new sources of financing. Under these conditions, compound interest rates decreased from 120 percent to 80 percent.

This decline certainly did not stem from the confidence in the economy, but from the liquidity supply by the Central Bank purchasing foreign currency. The Central Bank purchased foreign currency, and supplied the market with Turkish Lira. Thus, its reserves were strong enough not to allow any fluctuation. The growth rate of the debt stock weakened; however, this would not solve the basic problems. Yet, it helped to gain time in the short term.

However, it was not certain that the time was used efficiently. The growth rate of the economy after the economic crisis of 1994 was satisfactory, but the external equilibrium was defective. In the years 1995, 1996 and 1997, the Current Account Trade Balance demonstrating the foreign currency balance based on the commodities and services movements showed a deficit of more than US $2 billion.

The domestic balance, that is, the public sector balance was not at a budgetary equilibrium, even though the economy administration of the time claimed it to be. The economy was in a position of net consumer, and was facing problems in creating an added value. The improvement in the debt interest payments was benefited. Yet, even though the structural problems continued to exist, structural reform implementations were out of the question.

Table 1. Foreign Currency Balance of Turkey
(in US $ million)

Year	Foreign trade balance	Current account trade balance
1993	-14.160	-6.433
1994	-4,216	2.631
1995	-13.212	-2.339
1996	-10.582	-2.437
1997	-15.358	-2.638
1998	-14.220	1.984
1999	-10.443	-1.360

SOURCE: CBRT (CENTRAL BANK OF THE REPUBLIC OF TURKEY

The fiscal sector had serious problems as well. The 1994 economic crisis seriously damaged the banking system of which the capital adequacy and assets quality had deteriorated. The blanket guarantee protecting the bank deposits brought some relief after the crisis, but led to the appearance of numerous new banks. Thus, in a period where there was not sufficient and/or effective control, the banking sector went through an unhealthy growth. The Central Bank's foreign exchange rate surveillance with the help of its strong foreign exchange reserves encouraged the foreign exchange rate risk. Small- and medium-sized banks collected foreign currency at high interest rates. This foreign currency was then converted into Turkish Lira and placed in short position. The banks mainly purchased the government debt. This was the situation in early 1997. The expectations in the fiscal sector and international markets conformed to the idea that the system could not endure any longer. In January and February 1997, the interest rates increased from 80 percent to 110 percent once again, as a result of the release by a bank of its bond portfolio of US $200–250 million. The problem was that the market was not deep enough to tolerate even such a sale. There was a serious liquidity problem in the market.

In the meantime, there was an increasing political risk; the process of February 28 had just begun. In an environment of economic vulnerability, this development further increased the uncertainty, leading to a rise in the interest rates. February 28 was a sign of the coming elections. An economy of elections began to be implemented: base prices (set by the state for agricultural commodities) were rather high; additional rises in salary were offered to civil servants. However, the public sector had difficulties even in paying the government salaries, as observed in March and June 1997. The government resigned and a new minority government was established.

REALIZATION OF THE IMPORTANCE OF STRUCTURAL REFORMS

The structural reforms were put on the agenda after the establishment of the minority government. The executive board of the Treasury was changed. In compliance with the protocol signed between the Treasury and the Central Bank in August 1997, it was decided that the Treasury quit using short-term advances from the Central Bank. It was also emphasized that the state banks should not be included in the Treasury financing. Adoption of the primary dealership system was on the agenda; steps should be taken toward transparency; and the market should be deepened. Discussions on the necessity to restructure the fiscal system began in this period as well.

However, in November there was an impression that this process had been interrupted. Before November, in order to decrease the interest rates and combat inflation the Treasury got into debt to the market with the aim to close the advances used from the Central Bank. In July the fuel oil prices were raised, which would affect inflation. However, a positive result was expected by the public sector. Inflation would rise first and then it would decline gradually. The rise in the interest rates would affect the bond-holders first. The uneasiness in the economy was increasing. Inflation would be increased first, and then decreased gradually. At the beginning of 1998, it was declared that there would not be any price increase in the products of the State Economic Enterprises. Thus, there would be a significant decline in inflation in 1998. However, just before 1998, it was realized that the necessary steps toward structural reforms had not been taken. The Treasury Undersecretary resigned office for this reason.

The fiscal system continued to expose itself to more risks. High real interest rates encouraged the short position. In the second half of 1998, the economy administration directed the Central Bank to decrease the interest rates, leading to an increase in short position profits because the decline in the interest rates would increase the value of securities. It was obvious that the banks having in their portfolio Turkish Lira denominated securities would make profits. However, the banking system exposed itself to a serious risk; as a matter of fact, short position was a risk by itself. The banking sector continued to collect funds in the international markets through the structured financing method: bonds were given as a guaranty to the foreign banks, and loans two or three times higher than the guaranties were taken. A high foreign currency inflow (hot money) was realized in the second quarter of 1998 through this method. The liquidity wideness in the market decreased overnight interest rates to 40 percent from 60 percent; the bond compound interest rates declined to 70 percent from 150 percent. Hot money inflow raised optimism in the market. However, short positions continued to break records. On the other hand, the world was facing a crisis. The Asian crisis might spread to China. Japan and USA intervened in the markets to prevent panic, and the crisis caught Russia.

Russia was an important country in the emerging markets, and was considered in the same category as Turkey. Turkey would inevitably be affected by the Russian crisis. The fiscal system was exposed to high risks. A serious foreign currency inflow was provided through the structured financing method, and securities were given as a guaranty. The Russian crisis might cause a capital outflow from Turkey, and the prices of the securities might decline as a result of high interest rates during this outflow. In this case, the prices of the securities given as a guaranty would decline; therefore, the international finance houses would demand additional guaranties for the loans they had given. Yet the financial system carried on undertaking this risk. And the fears became real; after the Russian crisis, there was a serious capital outflow, and the interest rates reached 150 percent from 70 percent.

While the fiscal sector was experiencing unhealthy developments, the real sector could not get out of its habits. The real sector which had acquired the habit of living with inflation was in a rigid position due to its high stock and debt structure. However, the deflationist wave following the Asian and Russian crises disturbed to a great extent the real sector balance.

In the meantime, the Financial Millennium began to be discussed in Turkey. Despite its significance for Turkey, it was not a well-timed implementation. The budget was giving robust deficits which should be reduced by additional taxes. However, the independent adoption of the Financial Millennium would not work; it should be implemented as part of a larger reform. This was not the case though. It was later claimed that the cause of the capital outflow from Turkey was the Financial Millennium. However, the real cause was the Russian crisis. The capital outflow raised interest rates, and the banks funded the securities in their portfolio by repos at a rate of about 150 percent. Securities were purchased as well to prevent panics caused by the foreign capital outflow and by the sales of securities that had been given as a guaranty in the international markets. The aim was to prevent further increases in the interest rates, leading to large losses for the banks. In brief, the fiscal system was hard hit in 1998. The capital adequacy deteriorated; even though the costs were high, the assets were not healthy enough. There was an uncertainty about the soundness of credits, and the securities had already fallen in price.

While the CPI had been 91 percent and the WPI 99.1 percent in 1997, the CPI declined to 69.7 percent and the WPI to 54.3 percent in 1998. This was a deflationary period; even though the Turkish Lira was overvalued, a decline was observed in imports. Exports were problematic as well. However, the fiscal system's short position was an obstacle to a regulation in the foreign exchange rate. Therefore, the real sector was in a difficult situation as well. The fiscal system kept on undergoing an unstable growth, without making profits though. Banking service revenues were close to zero, and most of the banks were concerned to fund their corporate groups. The funds collected at high costs were transferred to certain corporate groups through the credits. The moral hazard experienced in the Asian banking system spread to the Turkish system as well. The blanket guarantee protecting the bank deposits formed the basis of this hazard. The profit maximization target was replaced by the target of proving strong enough to prevent bankruptcy. These factors also formed the basis of the financial crisis in November 2000. The crisis deepened within the system, and the assets quality and capital adequacy deteriorated in 1998. Yet, before this period the banks could partly transfer loans to the real sector, mainly to their corporate groups, and fund the Treasury. But now this was the end of the road.

The year 1998 was interesting in many ways: the Russian crisis, the Financial Millennium, the fall of the government in October. Interesting developments followed one after the other. In the second half of 1998, the broadcasting of "certain cassettes" led to some operations. Again in the second half of 1998, there was a serious armed conflict with the PKK, and relations with Syria were strained. However, at the end of 1998 "an invisible hand" intervened, and Turkey's external support began to increase substantially. A decisive attitude was assumed towards Syria: the PKK should leave Iraq, its leader should be returned to Turkey. Syria sent the PKK's leader, "Apo", outside the country. Russia was Apo's first stop, but Russia was dealing with the problem of Caucasus at that time. Thus, Apo was sent to Italy. The USA kept on supporting Turkey, and Apo could not take shelter in Italy either. He was then surrendered from Africa to the newly established Ecevit's minority Government. It was the beginning of 1999 and, the conditions were advantageous to Turkey.

However, the economy was not going well. Since 1989 the power had been in the hands of coalition governments and, vote maximization had become crucial. An uncertainty about the borrowing matter prevailed in the first months of 1999. Yet, unusual developments occurred in February. The surrender of Apo caused optimism in the country. Turkey would carry an election in April 18, and an inflow of capital to the market took place before the elections. On election eve, the interest rates declined, and the stock exchange index began to rise. Even though Turkey had many things to do, the finance became the most crucial factor in the economy. In the middle of the year, the economy was hard hit by the earthquake in August. The economic growth turned to negative because the industrial district was on the fault line, and production came to a halt. However, international solidarity came to the fore with the earthquake of August 17. Relations with Greece improved. The European Union had already accepted Turkey as a candidate. The IMF and World Bank declared that they would increase their support to Turkey because of the earthquake.

Just before the beginning of 2000, Turkey was accepted at the G-20 summit, and became a candidate to the EU; the summit of OSCE was held in Turkey; and a Stand-By Arrangement was made with the IMF. Turkey's importance on the international arena began to increase. From now on, politics, particularly world politics began to define the agenda.

Discussions on the line of Bakü-Ceyhan started in this period. Turkey accepted the Arbitration on the energy issue and, declared that she could supply the financing of this line. Thus, the thesis of some petroleum companies suggesting that the project was not feasible was eliminated. The risk of terrorism in the region was minimized after the surrender of Apo, the retreat of Syria, and the shift in the developed countries' preferences in the region.

The low oil prices were disturbing the countries in the region. USA war planes departed from Incirlik and hit the Yumurtalık-Kerkük pipeline. This meant a decrease by 2 million barrels in production. According to the decision of OPEC countries, there would be a decrease by 4.5 million barrels in production. Therefore, the oil prices increased from US $8 to US $17 per barrel.

1.2 Asian crisis and trends in the world economy and political structure

Let us analyze the changes in the Turkish economy and political structure since 1996 in parallel with those in the world economy and political structure, and find out the similarities.

The year 1996 was crucial for the United States. Bill Clinton won the elections for the second time. Clinton's first implementation was related to the budget deficit reduction. A program to be implemented within this framework would normally strengthen the US dollar. Subsequently the US dollar continued to appreciate during 1997. The US dollar which was equivalent to 1.47 Deutsche Mark by the end of 1996 was raised to 1.89 Deutsche Mark in 1997.

These developments affected, however, in a negative way the competitive power of those countries who had pegged their national currency to the US dollar – among them are the so-called "Asian Tigers", that is, Taiwan, Hong Kong, Indonesia, Malaysia and so on. The result was an increasing uncertainty in the markets and a decrease in the tendency to take risks. Foreign investors were worried and began to leave these countries. Thailand's foreign exchange reserves were insufficient for the outflow of foreign investment. Consequently, the Central Bank that ran out of foreign exchange reserves let the Thailand currency (Baht) float. Malaysia, Indonesia, Korea and Hong Kong experienced similar instances. The Asian crisis began to spread gradually through the world. This would lead to an increase in the problems around the world. In several export-based economies, the capacities were immediately increased; some of them were financed with foreign sources. The loss due to unproductive investments was mainly compensated with hot money. With the presumption that they could sell anything they produced, the real estate investments which could hardly be liquidated in these countries were put forward along with the investments to increase the production capacity by means of incoming foreign capital. However, the demand for export capacities did not increase immediately. The appreciation of the US dollar had a negative impact on the competitive power of these countries whose currency had been pegged to the US dollar. This fiscal policy and the risks that were taken resulted in a capital outflow and a dramatic increase in the foreign exchange rate, which would in turn cause the cash flow of the companies to deteriorate; the whole system came to a halt. The crisis began to spread throughout the world.

As a consequence of the Asian crisis, an imbalance was observed in the capital movements towards developing markets such as Turkey. The deflationary process which had evolved in Asia had a worldwide effect. The decreasing purchasing power and consumption level in Asia had a negative effect on the global demand, primarily on the demand for raw material. During this period Turkey continued to undergo high inflation.

In the second quarter of 1998 Turkey witnessed a significant foreign exchange inflow (hot money). However, the source of this inflow was short-term loans instead of sounder export and tourism revenues. Turkey ended up becoming in a sense a paradise of hot money. While the Asian crisis was expected to spread to China, it traveled to Russia despite the intervention by Japan and USA.

A decline in the demand for raw material, primarily for energy, and a decrease in the global demand as well led to a decrease in the prices of these inputs. Russia had a debt of US $16 billion – half of which were foreign debts – against a reserve of US $10–12 billion. Rumors which were circulated by foreigners that Russia necessitated US $10–12 billion led to a rise in the interest rates. Decreasing foreign exchange inflow and increasing interest rates caused a panic in Russia. At the summit of G7, it was suggested that Russia should sign a stand-by arrangement with the IMF which then would provide financial support to Russia. However, the initial negotiations between Russia and the IMF were unfruitful. Due to the insistence of G7, the IMF agreed to offer a credit of US $22.6 billion to Russia with an initial payment of US $4.9 billion. The expectations that Russia could not manage this debt properly created a panic, following a letter by Soros to the *Financial Times*. In consequence, Russia depreciated her currency on August 8, and put consolidation and moratorium on the agenda.

The only survivor of both the Asian and Russian crises was the USA with the least or maybe no loss. In fact the USA gained more power after these crises. In 1999 the European league tried to stand as an alternative power by introducing the Euro, but the USA was not comfortable with this development. The USA was very sensitive to the energy subject, and reacted to the bombing of the oil routes. As a world leader, she would certainly like to control the energy routes and fix energy prices. Her support for the Bakü-Ceyhan route was an indication of this. She should intervene in order to take control over the Caucasian oil. Europe was in political and economic chaos. Upon the capture of Apo, there were protests in Europe. In the meantime, a crisis in Brazil broke out. The Euro depreciated due to the Apo and Brazil crises.

A new world order was in action. The summit on July 23, 1999 about the financing of Kosovo was a turning point. After this summit, the tension between the USA and Europe seemed to be relieved. The USA reproached the Europeans for the delay in decreasing interest rates. Yet such adversities had no place in the new world order. Japan, on the other side had been struggling with numerous problems since 1990. She suffered serious losses in Asia, her banking system was problematic, and all deposits in the banks were protected by the state. Japan had no chance to resist the USA.

By the second half of 1999 astonishing events occurred, such as the acceptance of Turkey by G-20, the amendments in OSCE that was then held in Istanbul, and the agreement on Turkey's candidate status for EU membership.

Even though Turkey's candidacy for EU membership had been supported by the USA since February 1997, the EU's opinion was negative in mid-1998. Whatever had happened would be explained a year later: the USA had insisted on Turkey's candidacy, but it was rejected in Luxembourg. A year later, however, the light for Turkey was green. The new world order was in action. Turkey was in such a conjuncture at the beginning of 2000.

CHAPTER II

An analysis of the IMF program of 2000: why and how was it implemented?

2.1 Targets of the 2000 stabilization program and outline of the policies to be implemented

The Turkish Treasury Undersecretary stated the reasons and implementations of the 2000 program in the following order, in a letter dated December 9, 1999 submitted to the IMF Managing Director Michel Camdessus.

The goal of the program was determined as "freeing Turkey from inflation and enhancing the prospects for growth and for a better standard of living for all parts of society". The following points were noticed:

- Over the last 25 years, inflation has created instability in the economic growth. "Growth has not only been volatile, but has also been well below the average of the most successful emerging markets".

- "By undermining confidence in the Turkish lira, inflation has also resulted in high and unstable nominal and real interest rates (…). Speculative and arbitrage activities have attracted more and more resources, and have distorted the working of financial markets and institutions. When the government has to pay on its debt real interest rates of 30 percent or more, private capital moves away from job-creating activities into financial investment," and "the credit process is disrupted".

- "These high real interest rates, together with a weak fiscal primary position, have pushed public finances onto an unsustainable path". Public sector debt has increased from 44 percent of GNP at end-1998 to 58 percent of GNP at end-1999.

- Aggravating structural problems have not only increased inflation, but affected negatively Turkey's growth prospects in the long run.

THE GOALS OF THE DISINFLATION PROGRAM

With the aim to erase the negative effects of this process, the following goals are set:

Inflation target	GNP growth target	Current account balance target
• Inflation target for 2000 is projected to be by end-December 25 percent for CPI inflation, and 20 percent for WPI inflation. • Both WPI and CPI inflations are expected to decline to 10–12 percent by end-2001. • About 5–7 percent by end-2002	• GNP growth is projected to be in the range of 5–5½ percent in 2000. • GNP growth is expected to remain in the range of 5–6 percent in 2001 and 2002.	• The current account trade deficit is projected to increase to 1½–2 percent of GNP in 2000. • Deficits of the same order of magnitude are expected in 2001 and 2002.

The program had three main components on its way to reach the targets: "up-front fiscal adjustment, structural reform, and a firm exchange rate commitment (foreign exchange rate basket) supported by consistent incomes policies".

High public sector deficits were considered the ultimate factor behind high inflation. Thus, structural reforms were needed to make the fiscal adjustment sustainable and facilitate the decline of public sector debt. The public sector debt would be lowered by means of structural reforms and privatizations. On the other hand, a firm exchange rate commitment and consistent income policies were considered necessary to fight inflation. The details of the program were cited as the following:

FISCAL POLICY

In order to sustain public finances and to solve permanently the inflation problem, a substantial increase in the primary surplus of the public sector and an acceleration in privatizations were targeted. The fiscal policy was thus determined within this scope.

- In 1999 the primary balance of the public sector yielded a deficit of 2.8 percent of GNP. The fiscal goal for 2000 was to raise the primary surplus of the public sector from –2.8 percent to 3.7 percent of GNP (the latter figure excludes the privatization receipts, interest revenues, profit transfers from the Central Bank, and the expenses related to the earthquake). This would be sufficient to decrease the public sector debt. However, real interest payments on the securities issued at fixed interest rates in the past would increase as inflation fell, and this level of the primary surplus would not be sufficient. Thus, sizable privatization receipts were also needed to limit the growth of the public sector debt ratio. Yet the key question which had never been asked was to what extent it was reasonable to utilize privatization receipts as an income resource.

- The target set for privatization receipts was one of the most challenging targets of the 2000 program. They were expected to be 3.5 percent of GNP, that is, US $7.6 billion. The privatization receipts arising in the telecommunication and energy sectors (US $4½-5½ billion) would be transferred directly to the Treasury.

WHAT IS THE PRIMARY SURPLUS OF THE PUBLIC SECTOR?

The consolidated government sector within the program includes the consolidated central budget displaying the revenues and expenditures of the General and Annexed Budget Administrations, four key Extra-Budgetary Funds (EBFs), eight state economic enterprises, the unemployment insurance fund,

---

Graph 3. Domestic Debt Stock/GNP

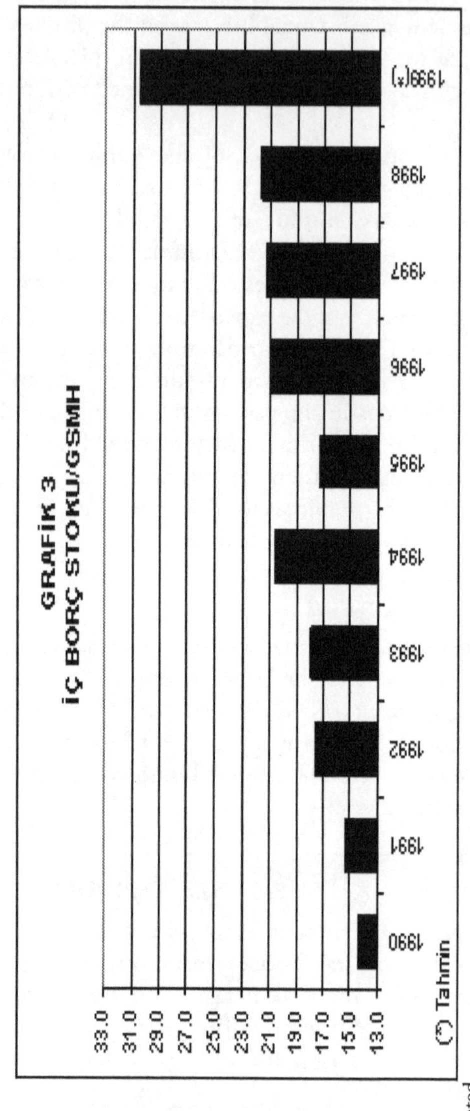

(*) Estimated

SOURCE: ERÇEL 6. GRAPH 3.

and the three social security institutions. The primary surplus of these institutions is projected to be 3.7 percent of GNP. For the consolidated budget, the primary surplus of the public sector is also called the surplus excluding interest expenditures. The primary surplus is equal to the total revenues of the consolidated budget minus non-interest expenditures. Thus, interest expenditures can be partially met by this surplus of the consolidated budget. If there is no primary surplus, the Treasury who is responsible for the expenditures and obligations of the consolidated budget becomes indebted for both the capital and its interest. In consequence, the public sector debt increases dramatically. Thus, the ratio of the public sector debt to the national income cannot be reduced.

- In order to reach the budgetary targets a tax package was necessary. A new tax package would come into effect. "This package includes additional personal income and corporate tax payments; an additional payment of the annual motor vehicle and property taxes; a tax on mobile phone bills; and an increase in the remittances of surpluses generated by regulatory boards (such as the Istanbul Stock Exchange, Capital Markets Board, and so on)". In addition, measures allowing individuals to reduce the duration of military service by payment of a fee were introduced, and a withholding tax on government securities issued before December 1, 1999 was in effect. These measures would raise revenues by about 2 percent of GNP. Yet there were more taxes to come: the withholding tax on income from fixed assets and on the self-employed, and the withholding tax on interest income from deposits and repos would be increased. With respect to indirect taxes, the standard VAT rate would be increased by 2 percentage points. In addition, oil price levies would be adjusted regardless of the behavior of oil price.
- Savings in the budget expenditure would be generated through cuts in noninvestment public expenditures, including savings from a reduction in personnel expenditure.
- Social security and agriculture reforms would be influential in savings. Expenditures would thus be put under control.

Graph 4. Consolidated Budget Balance and Primary Surplus (Ratio to GNP)

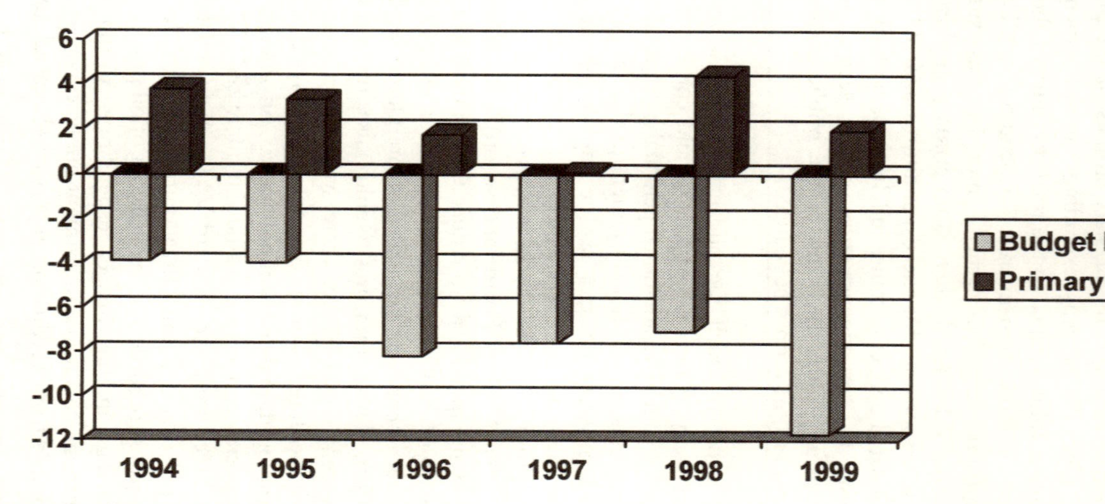

SOURCE: TT (TURKISH TREASURY)

- Finally, the total debt-to-GNP ratio was expected to decline slightly from 58 percent of GNP. Hence Turkey as a candidate of the EU would not exceed the EU maximum criterion of 60 percent. Privatization and public debt reduction targets would remain the same in 2001 and 2002.

Table 2. Privatization and Public Sector Debt

	Privatization Receipts / GNP (%)	Public Sector Debt / GNP (%)
2000	3.5	57.0
2001	3.25	56.5
2002	2	54.75

MONETARY AND EXCHANGE RATE POLICIES

Outlines of the monetary and exchange rate policies were as follows: "(...) disinflation and a rapid decline in interest rates require that monetary and exchange rate developments become more predictable, so as to reduce the uncertainty on the value of financial investment for both residents and nonresidents. This requires a shift to a more forward-looking commitment on exchange rate policy. The strengthening of fiscal policy under the program, our level of international reserves, coupled with the financial support from the international community, make the introduction of such a commitment feasible. (...) there is a need for a transparent and pre-announced exit strategy from this exchange rate regime". As seen above, the program of 2000 was based on a peg to the foreign currency, that is, on the predictability of the foreign exchange rate. The exchange rate path was announced: for the Turkish Lira basket composed of US $1 and Euro 0.77, the depreciation rate would be 20 percent, in other words the exchange rate increase was defined as 20 percent per basket. At the end of each quarter, the exchange rate basket increase would be pre-announced, and there would be no band around the exchange rate path. After the first eighteen months

Table 3. Foreign Exchange Basket and Foreign Exchange Rate Targets in 2000

	Basket value (end-month) (1 US $ + 0.77 Euro)		Basket Value Changes	
		Monthly increase rate (%)	Cumulative increase rate (%)	Daily increase rate (%)
December 1999	959,020.46			
January 2000	979,159.89	2.1	2.100	0.067
February	999,722.25	2.1	4.244	0.072
March	1,020,716.42	2.1	6.433	0.067
April	1,038,068.59	1.7	8.243	0.056
May	1,055,715.76	1.7	10.083	0.054
June	1,073,662.93	1.7	11.954	0.056
July	1,087,620.55	1.3	13.410	0.042
August	1,101,759.61	1.3	14.884	0.042
September	1,116,082.49	1.3	16.377	0.043
October	1,127,243.31	1.0	17.541	0.032
November	1,138,515.75	1.0	18.717	0.033
December 2000	1,149,900.90	1.0	19.904	0.032

SOURCE: ERÇEL 6. TABLE 1.

following the introduction of this regime, a symmetric, progressively widening band about the central exchange rate path would be introduced on July 1, 2001. The total width of the band would thus reach 7½ percent by end-December 2001, 15 percent by end-June 2002, and 22½ percent by end-December 2002.

Ceiling targets were set for the Net Domestic Assets (NDA) of the Central Bank. The NDA stock of the Central Bank at the end of each quarter would not exceed end-December 1999 level (minus Turkish Lira 1.2 quadrillion). However, short-run fluctuations in the range of ±5 percent of total base money at the end of the preceding quarter would be allowed. Finally, the reserve requirement coefficient applying to the stock of Turkish Lira deposits would be reduced from 8.0 percent to 6.0 percent and a liquidity requirement of 2 percent on Turkish Lira deposits, that is, on government domestic debt instruments would be imposed.

A floor performance criterion was set for the Central Bank on its Net International Reserves. The Net International Reserves which were US $17,900 million by end-September 1999 would decrease to US $12,000 million by end-December 1999, remain as US $12,000 million by end-March 2000, increase to US $12,750 million by end-June 2000, remain as US $12,750 million by end-September 2000, and increase to US $13,500 million by end-December 2000. Thus, the Central Bank reserves were targeted not to fall below a certain level.

Other than the short-term fluctuations, all Base Money (for definitions see the box entitled "The Central Bank balance sheet and the program of 2000"), that is, the Turkish Lira obligations of the Central Bank would be created through the bank's foreign exchange purchase which would be affected by the balance of payments, that is, the net amount of foreign exchange movements. The Central Bank's funding or liquidating of the public sector and/or the market was prevented by fixing the item of the Net Domestic Assets to minus Turkish Lira 1.2 quadrillion. The Central Bank would thus create Turkish Lira just through the purchase of foreign currency. However, foreign currency purchase by the market agents would reduce the TL supply in the market. Furthermore, since the Central Bank could only create

TL through the purchase of foreign currency, it could not supply the market with TL when necessary. Domestic interest rates would be fully market-determined. *What the market agents should be careful about was obvious: even though the program would eliminate the risk of foreign exchange rate, it would and could not take any measures to prevent the risk of interest rate.* All the market agents should have acted in light of this fact. When the Central Bank purchased foreign exchange, the interest rates could decrease dramatically. If the interest rates were to fall below 20 percent, the agents would then prefer to invest in foreign exchange, which would eventually decrease the TL supply in the market and increase the interest rates again. When the interest rates exceeded 20 percent, the agents would convert foreign exchange to TL, and the interest rates would fall again. Thus the market itself would determine the balance of interest rate. *The interest rate was in a sense the primary parameter in the program to resist the monetary shocks, in other words it was the fuse of the system.*

> ## THE BALANCE SHEET OF THE CENTRAL BANK AND THE PROGRAM OF 2000
>
> The balance sheet of the Central Bank has been revised within the framework of the IMF Stand-By Arrangement. The balance sheet is more clarified to monitor the relations between the items. As we already know, the analytical balance sheet of the Central Bank, that is, the balance sheet made to be analyzable, is divided into assets and liabilities. Under the assets are the Net Foreign Assets item consisting of foreign exchange assets (such as gold and foreign exchange) and the Net Domestic Assets item in TL (government domestic debt instruments, rediscount credits to banking sector, credits to the Saving Deposit Insurance Fund (SDIF)). The liabilities of the Central Bank are divided into total foreign currency liabilities consisting of foreign exchange liabilities in domestic and international markets, and TL liabilities consisting of currency issued, deposits of banking sector, extra- budgetary fund, deposits of non-banking sector, deposits of the public sector, open market operations and so on.

In the new balance sheet revised by the IMF, the assets consist of two items: Net Foreign Assets and Net Domestic Assets. As for the liabilities, there is Base Money.

Foreign assets are obtained by subtracting the Central Bank foreign exchange liabilities to non-residents and those to the banking sector from its foreign exchange assets. Domestic assets are obtained by subtracting deposits of the public sector from credits to the public sector and to the banking sector (including open market operations). Roughly speaking, since the foreign exchange liabilities are subtracted from the foreign assets (in foreign exchange), a single item remains in the assets: Base Money which comprises currency issued and banking sector's free deposits in TL and equivalent to TL kept in the Central Bank.

In the countries where the peg to foreign exchange is implemented, the IMF stipulates that the Central Bank domestic assets not exceed a certain level at a certain time and its foreign assets decrease to a certain level at a certain time.

STRUCTURAL REFORM

The structural reform was the most important part of the program because in order to attain a sustainable improvement, to sustain the macroeconomic balance in a steady way, to improve transparency and economic efficiency, and to reduce the contingent liabilities of the public sector, the implementation of structural reforms without any concession was crucial. Structural reforms were not only related to the public sector, but to the private sector as well.

Structural reforms in the public sector were categorized under different titles such as agricultural policies, pension reform, tax policy and administration, fiscal management and transparency.

Present agricultural support policies which had a burden of 3 percent of the GNP to the Treasury and which distorted resource allocation by distorting market price signals should be replaced by a cost-effective support system targeted at poor farmers. A Direct Income Support system would apply and a pilot program for the crop year 2000 would be set. In the interim, support prices would sustain. However, the new support system would be set gradually. The support prices for cereals in 2000 would be set such that the spread between support prices and the projected world market prices was no more than 35 percent of the projected c.i.f. world price, and reduced further in 2001. For sugar beet, similar implementations would apply. The agricultural sales cooperatives and their unions would operate within the framework of these principles.

The government would gradually phase out the credit subsidy to farmers. The total cost of credit subsidies sustained by Ziraat Bank and Halk Bank would decline from an estimated 1.2 percent of GNP in 1999 to 0.6 percent of GNP in 2000. The fertilizer and other input subsidies would remain constant in nominal terms in 2000 and 2001.

The social security system had begun to yield deficit due to a decrease in the minimum retirement age set in 1992. Supports provided to Bağkur, SSK, and Emekli Sandığı from the budget were 2 percent of GNP in 1998, and 2.8 percent in 1999. The total deficit of the social security system was 2.3 percent of GNP in 1998, and 3 percent in 1999. If no measures were taken, the deficit of the social security system would widen sharply from 3 percent of GNP to some 16 percent by 2050.

The first part of the comprehensive agenda for social security reform had been already completed by the parliament in September 1999: the minimum retirement age for new entrants was increased to 58/60 and to 52/56 for existing contributors over a ten-year transition period. The minimum contribution period for entitlement to a pension was raised, and the average replacement ratio was reduced from 80 percent to 65 percent; pension benefits were indexed to the CPI; and the ceiling on contributions was increased. The legal framework for private pension funds would be created. The reform appeared to be in parallel with the strict adoption of the decisions taken by the parliament in September.

As for the fiscal management and transparency, it includes the processes required "to strengthen budget preparation, execution, and control; to enhance transparency and accountability of fiscal operations". In this respect, 20 budgetary funds, out of a total of

61 budgetary funds, would be closed by February 2000; 25 more funds would be closed by August 2000. The remaining funds would be closed by June 2001. For the institutions subject to the consolidated central budget, an accounting and reporting system on a commitment basis would be introduced. Moreover, in 2001 an integrated financial information system based on a treasury single account and a general ledger would be implemented.

This reform was significant in enhancing transparency and accountability in budgetary operations. Duty losses of state banks consisting of credit subsidies and related costs would be included in the budget under the stock of liabilities; all government guarantees would be included under the stock of liabilities, making this information publicly available. The government would set explicit limits to issuance of new guarantees in the 2001 budget. Thus, the system aimed at limiting public-guaranteed loans by including EBFs in the budget.

Within the structural reforms, the improvement of the tax system and introduction of a tax system with a broad base and low and predictable marginal tax rates, along with clear laws and regulations were crucial to make the tax system more efficient and equitable. The transition to a full automation of the tax administration system that would enhance the effectiveness of the tax administration was the final stage of the tax reform.

Privatization was an integral part of the program. A regulatory body for the telecom sector would be established and all receipts from the privatization of Türk Telekom would be transferred to the Treasury shortly after the sale. The privatization program for 2000 had a challenging target of US $7.6 billion. These receipts were expected to come from the sale of 20 percent of Türk Telekom to a strategic investor, as well as two wireless licenses, the TOR for electricity distribution and power plants. The sales by the Privatization Agency of 51 percent of Petrol Ofisi and of 15 percent of Tüpraş were among the performance criteria.

In order to improve domestic debt management, primary dealers in government securities markets would be introduced. Primary dealers would be committed to quote two-way prices and participate in government securities auctions. This would bring the Turkish government securities market in line with the practice of most EU countries, and would enhance its liquidity.

Strengthening the banking system and banking regulation were the most significant reforms other than the reforms in the public sector. In order to reduce interest rates and improve economic efficiency, the fiscal system needed to be improved. In late September, the limit on commercial banks' net open foreign position was lowered to 20 percent of capital. However, some important weaknesses remained on this issue. In June 1999, parliament had approved a new banking law that *inter alia* had created a new supervision authority (the Banking Regulation and Supervision Agency or BRSA). The BRSA was made fully autonomous in decision making and execution. The transfer of all insolvent banks to the SDIF was among the duties of the BRSA. The new amendments would give the SDIF the authority and responsibility to restructure a problem bank to facilitate its sale in full or in part, or to liquidate the remainder based on existing laws. The said institution would also be responsible for increasing transparency, strengthening key prudential regulations, and providing all of the tools needed for the improved resolution of problem banks. The Board of the BRSA would be named by end-March 2000.

To guide the private sector to set wage and price increases in line with the inflation target was crucial for the success of the program. To this end, the government would play an active role in the negotiations between the social sides. The government would be in close communication with the trade unions and employers. After the approval of the Economic and Social Council Law in April, this correspondence would continue.

2.2 Why did the program prove unsuccessful?

The program of 2000 was the most comprehensive program in Turkish economic history. The targets were challenging. In mid-1998 a Staff Monitoring Agreement – in which the need for a structural reform had been discussed as well – was signed with the IMF. However, the decision taken in spring 1999 about coming elections had a negative effect on the realization of this program. Nevertheless, the new coalition government had decided on a new and comprehensive program at the end of 1999, and signed a Stand-By Arrangement with the IMF. International public opinion was also in favor of the implementation of a new program for Turkey (see the previous section for the developments on this subject). Turkey had signed sixteen stabilization programs with the IMF. What was the difference of this one? Time would show. The program started at a rapid pace in terms of the legal amendments. The necessary legal infrastructure was nearly completed before April 2000. In this respect, the parliament passed the test. However, of crucial importance was the realization of the program.

The program had some basic targets:

- Public financing deficits and related financing methods were considered as the primary causes of the inflation in Turkey, and these financing needs were projected to be minimized by means of a fiscal policy based on a fiscal discipline. Therefore, a decrease in the high nominal and real interest rates would be attained as a result of the declining inflation and public financing needs.

- In order to achieve a sustainable decrease in the public financing needs, structural reforms (such as social security reform, agricultural reform, public sector reform, privatization, fiscal sector reform) would immediately be carried out.

- In parallel with the decline of high interest and inflation rates, the primary public surplus target when combined with decreasing public financing needs would lead to a reduction in the ratio of public sector debt to GNP.

- The Central Bank adopted the peg to foreign currency with the aim to decrease inflation. Thus, the inflation which had risen in parallel with increasing exchange rates for years (see the following graph) and the expectations would be put under control, and the inflationary inertia would be broken down.

- With the new program, the backward indexation and foreign exchange rate-based savings alternatives would be affected as well.

Graph 5. Wholesale Price Index and the Basket Peg (Annual Change In Percent)

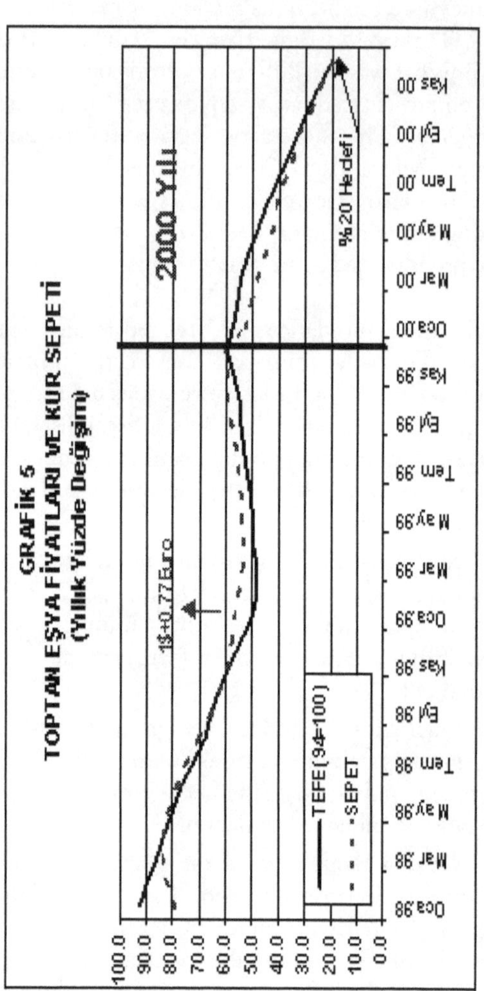

SOURCE: ERÇEL 6. GRAPH 5.

Why then did such a widely accepted program fail? And why was the peg replaced by the floating exchange rate regime? The following section explores the answers to these questions.

A GENERAL OVERVIEW

The crucial problem with this program was that it was not properly explained to the public. This technically detailed program should have been discussed by all the interested parties of society who could finally have come to a consensus. However, it was not the case. Everyone interpreted it as he or she wished.

In the peg regime, the interest rates would inevitably decline since the exchange rate risk was eliminated. However, the decrease in interest rates was not properly assessed by the economy administration, primarily by the fiscal sector. The general view was that in the peg system interest rates would decline in a continuous way. However, no one had elaborated on what should be avoided to ensure the sustainability of this tendency, and society was left uninformed. The real problem emerged from the fiscal system itself, and from the public sector who obeyed the policies of the fiscal system.

The fiscal sector (banks and other financial intermediaries) interpreted the program on the speculation that the foreign exchange rate was eliminated and that the decrease in interest rates would continue; the sector then took positions accordingly. However, in order to achieve a sustainable decrease in the interest rates within the program, a net capital inflow was needed. Otherwise, the program was doomed to fail. Nevertheless, the fiscal sector acted without facing the truth: short-term funds should be collected; people should retain their savings in foreign currency; the fiscal sector itself, on the other hand, should convert its assets into long-term assets (these were the reasons for the trend towards consumer credits and the government domestic debt instruments portfolio) and take short position. Large profits could thus be made under these conditions of decreasing interest rates and nonexistent foreign exchange rate risk. Hence, their melted capitals could be (in a sense) reestablished.

The economy administration acted in a similar manner. While the interest rates were going down, the Treasury could find loans with lower costs; and as the economy would grow due to decreasing interest rates, the ratio target of the public debt to the national income would be met without needing structural reforms and tight budget policies. It was assumed that there was no problem as long as the economy was kept growing and that the debts were managed with tolerable costs. However, no meticulous evaluation had been made on the sustainability of the conditions.

The decreasing interest rates would certainly revive the economy. Consumption which was supported with consumer credits began to increase. The savings rate was on the other hand declining. In such a case where the economy growth was based on domestic demand, imports and thus the foreign trade deficit would certainly increase. The revival of the economy would result in an inflation rate exceeding the foreign exchange rate, which would lead to an appreciation of the Turkish Lira. Therefore, the external deficit widened. While Turkey was expecting a net capital inflow, she had to finance the deficit with hot money. Uncertainty and vulnerability began to increase with the hot money factor. However, one could never predict when and how the hot money would escape. Hence, when the net capital outflow could not be prevented everything turned into a nightmare…

2.2.1   High inflation and high interest rates which had prevailed in Turkey for many years brought along a tendency to backward indexation. There was an attempt to compensate the insufficient savings deficit with hot money. Therefore, the debt was further increasing while the real interest rate was at a high level. The public sector was the sector which used nearly all the savings. From the early 1990s, there existed a fiscal system which was accustomed to earn money from hot money, and reluctant to get out of this habit. Savings were not invested in a proper way due to this tendency of the fiscal system. There was a serious currency substitution. High inflation was triggering this process because there was a lack of confidence in the domestic currency. This situation was abused by the fiscal system. People's money would stay in foreign currency; the fiscal system would, however, convert these foreign currency deposits into Turkish Lira investments. This fact called short position sustained during the implementation of the program. The vicious circle could not be broken. Change and restructuring were doomed to stay just as words, and were not applied in real life.

THE CURRENCY SUBSTITUTION LEVEL IN TURKEY: The currency substitution level in Turkey was disastrous before the program. The breakdown of M2Y (broad money) – which is money supply in a generic sense, and which comprises the Turkish Lira in circulation (bills + coins) plus Turkish Lira deposits and foreign currency accounts – was striking at the end of 1999; 56.1 percent of M2Y was foreign currency accounts. This share decreased to 51.3 percent by September 2000; however, it reached 57.4 percent at the end of 2000.

2.2.2   In an environment where there was foreign exchange rate risk, it was natural to expect high yield from national currency. When this situation came along with public sector deficits and financing, the result was high nominal interest rates.

2.2.3   The peg regime eliminated the foreign exchange rate risk. As mentioned in the previous section, the Central Bank committed to a foreign exchange rate increase of 20 percent in 2000 on the base of an exchange rate basket composed of US \$1 + Euro 0.77. Furthermore, a comprehensive program was introduced. This decision would naturally be reflected in the interest rates. Since the foreign exchange rate risk was eliminated – which had been the most important risk determining the TL interest rates – nominal interest rates were supposed to decrease immediately.

2.2.4   Let me emphasize a point here: in economies with free capital movements, if the Central Bank commits to the foreign exchange rate, it will then set the interest rate free. Likewise, if it sets the foreign exchange rate free, it will then be able to hold the interest rate. All the economic units should be on the alert for this principle called the Impossible Trinity. The Central Bank had committed to the foreign exchange rate, but announced that the interest rate would be determined by the market conditions.

2.2.5   The basic goal of the program which was to achieve an immediate decrease in the nominal and real interest rates and to keep them at a low level, appeared to be in contradiction with the market-defined interest rates. However, a sustainable decrease in the interest rates might be attained with an unproblematic balance of payments and a direct inflow of foreign capital. On the other hand, a ceiling for the Net Domestic Assets of the Central Bank was set by the IMF, and this target should not be exceeded. Under this condition, the Central Bank could not supply the market with liquidity with the aim to decrease interest rates. Only an improvement in the balance of payments and a net foreign capital inflow might have caused a decrease in the interest rates. Liquidity would emerge in such a case because the Central Bank would purchase foreign currency from the market, and the interest rates would then begin to decrease. This process should be based on a strict discipline because the decreasing interest rates might stimulate consumption, leading to a larger consumption than the income. Incomes were projected to decrease within the framework of the structural reforms; in the meantime, consumption should be put under control. The essence of the program was based on savings.

2.2.6   With the implementation of the program, a decrease in the interest rates was unavoidable (see 2.3). This decrease would then affect the equilibrium between consumption and savings. From the very beginning of the program, most probably due to the enduring memory of inflation and interest rates, the decrease in the nominal interest rates caused an increase in consumption and a decrease in savings.

2.2.7   A noteworthy feature of the program was that Turkey needed savings; however, this aspect remained unintelligible. People should have been advised that particularly with the implementations of 2001, the situation would worsen, causing unemployment, and that savings would be of great necessity in

Graph 6. Decreasing Savings Widened the Current Account Deficit (The Ratio to GNP)

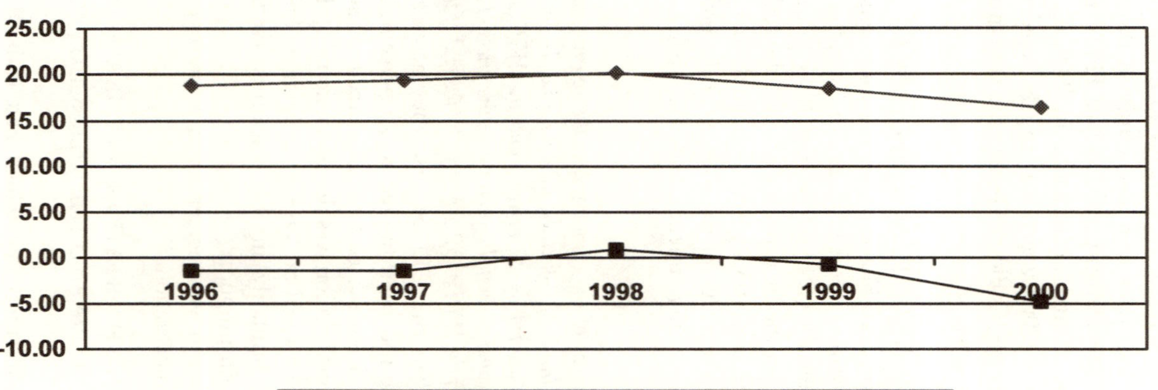

this process. It was indeed difficult to orient people to savings while the interest rates were declining; yet this fact should have been explained to a larger part of society. However, this was never done in practice. After a contraction in 1999, the rapid growth of the economy in 2000 which was largely based on consumption and consumer credits did not bother the government at all, and it was used as a source of praise.

2.2.8. In 1999 the GNP had decreased by 6.1 percent, and the GDP by 4.7 percent. However, the economy began to revive with the implementation of the program. In 2000, the GDP realized as 7.2 percent, and the GNP 6.1 percent. If we inspect the figures on quarter-basis, in the first quarter of 2000 the real growth was 4.2 percent, in the second 5.4 percent, in the third 7.2 percent, and in the last 7.8 percent. As for the sources of the growth, 3.8 percent of them were investment, and 5.3 percent consumption expenditures.

2.2.9. The revival of the economy and the consumption-based economic growth would inevitably affect the inflation rate. In the program of 2000, the CPI was targeted as 25 percent, and the WPI as 20 percent. The revival in the economy created a pressure on the prices. The CPI realized as 39 percent, and the WPI as 32.7 percent by the end of the year. The WPI was lower than the CPI because the increase in the foreign exchange rate had been limited to 20 percent. Imported inputs were provided with a cost of 20 percent. The uncontrollable increase in consumption was the alarm signal of the program. The credit stock had a real increase of 20 percent. The increase in the credit stock, primarily in the consumer credits, substantially supported consumption. However, the consumption-based economic growth was perceived as a positive process by the economy administration.

IMPACT OF HIGH INFLATION ON THE APPRECIATION OF THE TURKISH LIRA AND THE BALANCE OF PAYMENTS

2.2.10 The inflation rate which had realized over the target resulted in the appreciation of the Turkish Lira. At the beginning of the program in 2000, the TL had a higher value of 25 percent in terms of CPI and of 10 percent in terms of WPI, than its values in 1995, according to the figures given by the Central Bank. The exchange rate was not increased at the beginning of the program. *When the TL entered the program, it had already appreciated.* The reasons of the appreciation of TL were mainly political, such as the promises given to the IMF that the program would be strictly implemented and the reforms would be performed, and the USA's stance in favor of an agreement between the IMF and Turkey. However, the exchange rate increase for 2000 was projected as 20 percent, and the inflation rate was obvious. In 2000 the TL appreciated by 48 percent in terms of CPI, and by 18 percent in terms of WPI when compared with the figures of 1995. The TL was overvalued. A natural reflection of this situation would appear in the balance of payments, in other words in the current account trade balance.

2.2.11. The overvaluation of the national currency affected the foreign account deficit negatively: while the export (FOB) had been realized as US $26.5 billion in 1999, it was US $27.0 billion in 2000; however the import (in terms of CIF value) increased to US $54.5 billion from US $40.6 billion in one year. The foreign trade deficit which had been realized as US $10.4 billion in 1999 increased up to US $22.3 billion in 2000. The foreign trade deficit was so large that it was impossible to decrease it by means of the service sector revenues such as tourism receipts and workers' remittances. While the current account balance deficit had been US $1.3 billion in 1999, it increased up to US $9.8 billion, that is, to 4.9 percent of GNP in 2000. A solution had to be found to decrease the deficit.

2.2.12. If the Current Account Trade Balance yields a deficit, the alternatives of financing it are known: this deficit should be compensated with foreign source (debt) and/or international reserves. With the aim to decrease the deficit amounting to US $9.819 billion in 2000, a foreign source comprising short-, medium- and long-term debts and totaling US $9.445 billion was found; US $112 million of it was direct investment, and US

$1.022 billion portfolio investment. In addition, the IMF provided in 2000 a credit amounting to US $3.351 billion. The total foreign source inflow was US $12.796 billion; however US $9.819 billion was used to decrease the foreign trade deficit, and only an amount of US $354 million was added to the international reserves. The remaining US $2.623 million (net errors and omissions) escaped out of the system due to uneasiness.

PUBLIC SECTOR DEFICITS AND THE SUSTAINABILITY OF FINANCING

2.2.13 *The reasons for the deterioration of the balance of payments cannot be solely summarized as the increase in consumption, the decrease in domestic savings, and the appreciation of the Turkish Lira.* One of the most significant reasons for this deterioration was the high public sector deficits. When domestic savings cannot compensate the public sector deficit, deficits in the foreign balance come out. In an environment where the interest rates decline dramatically, the tendency to make savings decreases, leading to a deterioration in the mechanisms necessary to reduce the public sector deficit.

2.2.14 In order to reveal whether the 2000 program which was implemented to decrease the public sector deficit was based on a strict discipline, the ratio of the consolidated budget expenditures and revenues to the GNP should be assessed. While the ratio of the consolidated budget expenditures to the GNP had been 33.8 percent in 1999, it increased to 37.3 percent in 2000. There was also an increase in the share of the consolidated budget revenues. This ratio which had been 22 percent in 1999 increased to 27 percent in 2000. In other words, the public sector seemed to have a continual increase during 2000. However, in reality, it attempted to increase its revenues with the aim to decrease the deficit. The result was not satisfactory: the ratio of the consolidated budget deficit – which is the difference between the revenues and expenditures of the General and Annexed Budget Administrations – to the GNP was decreased to 10.3 percent in 2000 from 11.8 percent in 1999. However, the total deficit of the public sector, comprised of primarily the social security institutions, the

Graph 7. Public Sector Deficit and Domestic Debt Stock (The Ratio to GNP)

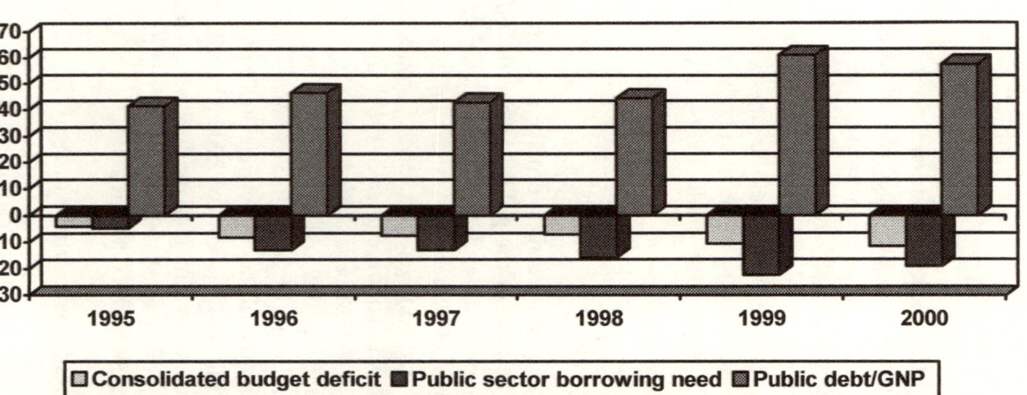

SOURCE: TT

state economic enterprises, local administrations, and funds, was disastrous. The ratio of the total deficit of the public sector to the GNP had increased to 22.3 percent in 1999; this ratio realized as 19.2 percent in 2000 with no substantial decrease. The level of the public sector deficit was alarming.

2.2.15   According to the Maastricht criteria of the EU, the ratio of the budget deficit to the GNP should be less than 3 percent, and the ratio of the public debt to the GNP less than 60 percent. The EU countries as well have problems in realizing these ratios; however Turkey's problem is more critical. First, as long as the budget is not radically amended, the ratio of the budget deficit to the GNP is doomed to remain at a high level. To attain a sustainable decrease in the public debt is indeed one of the main goals of the program.

WAS THE PROGRAM OF 2000 SUCCESSFUL IN DECREASING THE PUBLIC DEBT?

2.2.16   At this point we should make a general overview of the debt stock. The ratio of the public debt to the GNP was realized as 71.1 percent as of end-1999. This ratio decreased to 68.6 percent in 2000. However, the real picture is a bit different. First, the economy had contracted in 1999. Second, the duty losses of the state banks were not included in the figures of 2000. Likewise, the duty losses were not included in the figures of the previous years. Nevertheless, the loss amount displayed a higher increase under the conditions of 2000. For instance, while the duty losses were TL 13.5 quadrillion by March 2000, they increased to TL 17.279 quadrillion at the end of 2000; they further increased to TL 25.038 quadrillion in 2001 with a net increase of TL 7.759 quadrillion. In other words, there was no real decrease in the ratio of the public debt to the GNP in 2000.

2.2.17   Domestic debts amounting to TL 22.9 quadrillion had reached 29.3 percent of the GNP in 1999. In 2000 with an amount of TL 36.4 quadrillion excluding duty losses, the domestic debt corresponded to 29 percent of the GNP. In brief, the 2000 program was unsuccessful in meeting the target set for decreasing the public debt.

Table 4. Course of the Domestic Debt
(excluding duty losses, in TL trillion)

	1995	1996	1997	1998	1999	2000
Domestic Debt	1.361	3.149	6.283	11.613	22.920	36.420

SOURCE: TT

2.2.18   The maturity structure and content of the domestic debt stock were as important as the amount of the stock. By December 2000, the breakdown of the domestic debt was as follows: 8 percent was foreign currency-indexed borrowing, 35 percent was borrowing on the base of variable interest, and 56 percent was borrowing on the base of fixed interest. In a period when it was attempted to decrease the inflation rate, the proportion of borrowing on the base of fixed interest was rather high. Under such conditions, the Treasury would inevitably pay high real interest. Hence, the target of decreasing the ratio of the public debt to the GNP was in contradiction with the type of borrowing. As for the maturity of the debt, it was shorter in 2000 than in 1999, but longer than one year on average.

SOURCE: PROGRAM OF 2002

Deposit account interests stand for simple interests given for a three-month maturity deposit. The interests of government domestic debt instruments are compound interests. The interests of the interbank monetary market are compound interests; but for November 2000 and February 2001 these interests are displayed as simple interests for a clearer graph. However, the interbank interest rate realized in compound interest as 627.3 percent in November 2000, and 7525.7 percent in February 2001.

2.2.19   We must admit that the public sector took decisive steps toward improvement in 2000 when compared to 1999. A relative improvement was indeed observed in the first half of the year as a result of the efforts at reform, the public sector surplus target, and a relief in the budget due to the interest rates which decreased thanks to the foreign support provided for the program (such as export of 30– and 10–year bonds). However, what was important was the sustainability of this situation. For this reason, structural

Graph 8. Course of the interest rates (%) before the stabilization program and after its implementation

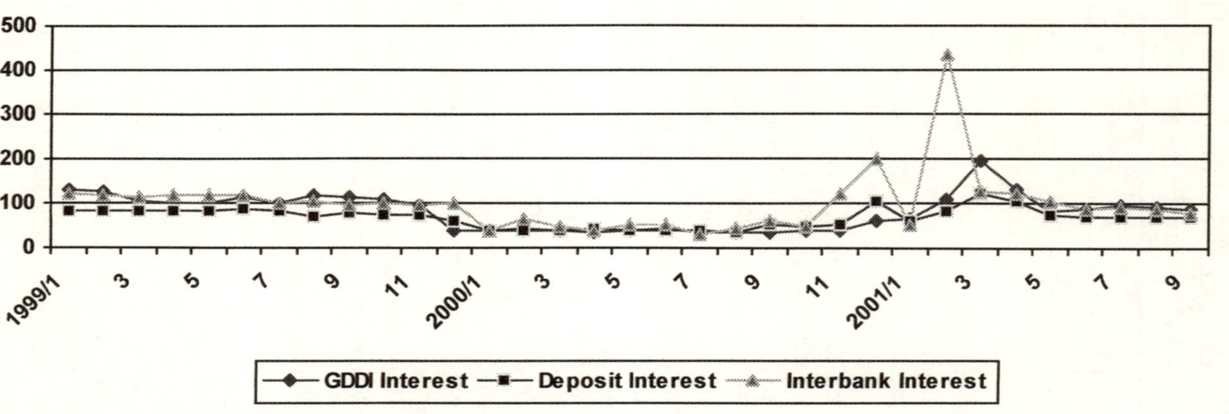

reforms needed to be realized properly, taking Turkey's condition into account as well. Suspicions about the adequacy of the reforms began to emerge in 2000 and later, due to the gradual increase in the deficit of the social security system, and the implementation of the agricultural reform with a tendency to support usually the non-productive sector instead of the producer. On the other hand, a long period of time was needed in order to bring the public sector deficit under control and to reduce the total public sector deficit, primarily budget deficit, to reasonable levels. In the meantime, the economy was to keep growing, real interest rates decline, and the public sector continue to yield a high-rated primary surplus (a rate of 3.6 percent excluding privatization and earthquake expenditures). Could the economy go through this period without crisis and reach the targets?

2.2.20 If the pros and cons of the contents of the reform package had been weighed up in detail, its implementation would have been smoother. However, reform efforts and related structural arrangements in 2000 were all prepared with a focus on the World Bank and the IMF, and were imposed upon society. For instance, at the second half of the year, disagreements on the legal arrangements concerning the privatization of the state banks began to emerge between the Government and the President. Serious delays were observed in the implementation of the fiscal sector reform which was one of the key areas of the program, and in the takeover of duty by the Banking Regulatory and Supervisory Agency (BRSA). BRSA finally took up its duty at the end of August. Public expectations became negative as a result of the discussions on Telekom and state banks. Even 50 percent of the privatization target of US $7.6 billion was not expected to be met. Hence, the privatization realized under US $3 billion in 2000. This figure was rather high, but not even 50 percent of the target. However, the public sector area of the program was based on expenditure reduction, income increase and privatization.

2.2.21 The negative effects caused by decreasing interest rates on consumption and hence on inflation could only have been avoided if the pros and cons of the program had been explained to the public and if the institutions had acted within this framework. The weakest feature of the program was its inability to cope with the increasing inflation due to the boom in consumption. In an environment where an increase of 20 percent was committed for the foreign exchange rate, the TL might appreciate causing a negative effect on the current account deficit. Hesitation on this issue was expressed by the IMF as well: measures should be taken to restrict domestic demand. For this reason, the rate of the Resource Utilization and Support Fund in consumer credits was increased to 8 percent from 4 percent. In order to cut the demand for luxury cars, the rate of VAT was increased. The tendency in the markets began to change by September. The measures were late; the IMF did not release the third portion of the credit to Turkey, and delayed it to December.

DEVELOPMENTS AFFECTING THE FISCAL SYSTEM AND THE EMERGENCE OF THE LIQUIDITY CRISIS

2.2.22   Let us analyze here the fiscal system, and hence the banking system. By the beginning of 2000, several legal arrangements in the banking system were put on the agenda. The aim was to create a banking system conforming to the new legislation and to the international arrangements and recommendations. Risk management and preparation of consolidated fiscal tables were now obligations to fulfill. The regulatory agency was provided with full authority over the insolvent banks, and limitations were put on the establishment of new banks and on the opening of new branch offices.

2.2.23   By end-1999 the Saving Deposit Insurance Fund had taken over five private trade banks and ceased the operations of a development bank and an investment bank. Thus, the number of banks transferred to the Fund increased to eight. As a result of the developments in 2000, three more private trade banks were transferred to the Fund. Two development and investment banks' operations were ceased during this period.

2.2.24   We know that, as a result of the financial liberalization in 1989, the banking system had tended to take risks, that the foreign capital share in its source had rapidly increased, and that off-shore banking had begun to operate. We further know that the system had suffered a severe stroke, and that the banks which had taken short position (who had borrowed foreign currency and converted it in TL instruments) had experienced heavy losses. In 1994, in order to prevent withdrawals from bank accounts, the Treasury had offered a blanket guarantee protecting the bank deposits, and thus, undertaking the banks' risks. After this period, numerous new banks had begun to appear.

Table 5. Quantitative Outlook of the Banking System

	1995	1999	2000
Number of Banks	68	81	79
Number of Branch Offices	6.244	7.691	7.837
Number of Personnel	144.793	173.988	170.401

SOURCE: BAT (BANK ASSOCIATION OF TURKEY)

2.2.25   The rapid increase in the number of new banks and branches was closely linked to the blanket guarantee protecting bank deposits. "Moral hazard" was also an important factor in the efforts to establish a new bank. The bank's assets were transferred for the owner's sake illegally, particularly through the approval of credits for illegitimate applicants. All the countries where the bank deposits are put under the Treasury guarantee have had similar experiences. Japan is an illustrative example.

2.2.26   The repayment of the sources collected with a high cost would probably be problematic. However, we should admit that the public authority had allowed all these developments, or covered them up in a sense. Private trade banks whose assets' structure was spoiled to a great extent, attempted to generate revenues "generally" by funding the public sector through the purchase of government domestic debt instruments; on the other hand, the credits offered by these banks were substantially used as a "capital" by their "own" corporate groups. The quality of the credits was out of the question. Banks attempted to make profits by taking high risks of foreign exchange, that is, by taking short position. Otherwise, they would not be able to compensate the high costs of the funds they had collected. The public authority did not recognize the fact that the number of banks was in contradiction with the savings in Turkey. The reason was clear: the public authority was in favor of these institutions which helped it manage its debts. Nothing left to be done. The system would collapse in the next step.

OUTLOOK OF THE FISCAL SYSTEM BEFORE THE NOVEMBER 2000 CRISIS FROM THE VANTAGE POINT OF BRSA

Banks

- Liquidity problems
- Overnight obligations of the state banks reaching to US $14 billion
- High short positions of the private banks
- High share of the public sector bonds in the banks' balance sheets
- Low assets' quality
- Insufficient risk assessment and risk management systems
- Nonexistence of a good corporate governance

Factors affecting the sector

- Severe economic instabilities.
- High deficits of the public sector.
- Systemic deformities stemming from the state banks and problematic banks.

SOURCE: BRSA (BANK REGULATION AND SUPERVISION AGENCY

2.2.27 At the beginning of 2000, the equity capital of the banking system began to melt down, which brought up the capital inadequacy as one of the serious problems of the sector. Similar developments were observed in 2000. The equity capital profitability which realized under the inflation rate implied the melting down of the equity capital in real terms. Even though there are doubts about whether the announced profits are in real terms or not, the following table offers an idea of the inflation rate and equity capital profitability.

Table 6. Comparison of the banks' equity capital profitability (net profit/equity capital) with inflation (%)

	1998	1999	2000
Private Commercial Banks	60.9	52.0	11.5
State Banks	16.2	38.1	-18.6
Total Banking System	37.5	-10.9	-68.4
CPI	69.7	68.8	39
WPI	54.3	62.9	32.7

SOURCE: BAT

2.2.28   In an environment of high inflation and high interest rates, the banks will inevitably reflect their inefficiency on the prices, and/or will rely on short-position profits. For instance, while the ratio of the banks' operations costs to their total assets was 4.8 percent between 1995 and 1999 on annual average, a maximum of 2.8 percent was generally set for this ratio in the world. In the country report published in 1999 on this subject, the IMF had compared Turkey's banking system with those of other countries, and had reported that the Turkish banks were working inefficiently and that they would be confronted with serious problems if the high inflation and interest rates process ended. Another problem of the banks was the "structured financing".

2.2.29   High short-term interest rates and the controlled gradual increase of the foreign exchange rate since 1998 led banks and foreigners who were reluctant to take risks to a different type of financing. A new alternative method to repo emerged: finding loans in the international markets by offering government domestic debt instruments as a guarantee. These loans were generally utilized in the domestic market which was characterized by decreasing interest rates in two ways: purchase of government domestic debt instruments and consumer credit. Some of the credits were transferred to the state banks through the interbank market. These foreign credits were offered on the condition that the banks would immediately meet new guarantee demands if the market "price" of the guarantees decreased. Otherwise, these guarantees would be liquidated and the credits offered would be re-collected regardless of a maturity condition. As a result, the liquidity crisis emerged.

2.2.30   The stabilization program which was implemented at the beginning of 2000 started at a rapid pace. Legal arrangements were immediately made. However, doubts started to be raised about the implementation by the second half of the year. Heated discussions on the decree related to the state banks and on the privatization of Telekom were going on. Consumption was increasing irrationally, and future incomes were mortgaged to meet consumption expenditures supported by consumer credits. When decreased savings due to increased consumption came along with high public sector deficits, it was figured out that the current account trade deficit would realize over the expected figure. The problem of funding fund banks was aggravating. Duty losses reached high levels in the state banks' assets. Before September 2000, foreigners had perceived the jeopardy. The overvalued TL would result in a robust current account deficit. In addition, the foreign currency short position of the banks in their balance sheets reached US $18 billion. The short position level of the private sector and other finance houses could not even be determined. Under these conditions, the Central Bank might not meet its foreign exchange rate commitment. Foreigners first began to sell eurobonds. Eurobond prices began to decrease in the international markets. In the domestic market, the same would occur for the government domestic debt instruments. Foreigners were asking new guarantees since the market price of the existing guarantees decreased. With the aim to fulfill their obligations, the banks should liquidate their assets and then purchase foreign currency with this TL in order to complete guarantees. However, they could not collect the money given to the state banks because duty losses were funded with this money. It was impossible to call in consumer credits. Other credits would be called in or these institutions would accept high interest rates. Credits quality was already problematic, which made it difficult for the banks to collect funds in short term. The last solution was the sale of the government domestic debt instruments. However, several private commercial banks were in the same situation. Therefore, the government domestic debt instrument market was locked in a sense; it was getting difficult to liquidate the government domestic debt instruments. There were no purchasers or they were in a very limited number. For instance, 10 percent of the government domestic debt instruments was in Demirbank's portfolio and Demirbank was the most significant primary dealer. Banks rushed into the repo, and the repo rates began to increase rapidly. Foreigners were converting their money from TL to foreign currency, while the banks were attempting to complete their guarantees by converting the money they had collected from TL to foreign currency. Since the Central Bank had a foreign currency commitment, it should sell the foreign currency requested by the market. International reserves decreased by US $6.3 billion in November. The Net International Reserves floor target by the end of the year was US $13.5 billion, and the critical level had already fallen below. Foreign credit corporations began to place pressure on the Turkish banks which were facing difficulties in investing new guarantees. What the foreigners requested was no longer the completion of guarantee but the closing of the credits. How could the banks – which had difficulties even in completing the guarantee – close the credits? Due to the increasing interest rates, the market price of government domestic debt instruments within their assets was reduced to one third. There was a serious problem. On the one hand, insufficient liquidity was rapidly worsening the financial structures of the banks. On the other hand, foreigners were urging them to close the credits. The transfer of Demirbank to the Saving Deposit Insurance Fund was on the agenda. In order to overcome the November panic, the Treasury had to offer guarantee to credits collected in international markets. All the obligations of the banks were henceforth under the Treasury guaranty.

COULD THE CENTRAL BANK HAVE PREVENTED THE LIQUIDITY CRISIS?

2.2.31   The answer to this question can be a simple "yes." The Central Bank could have certainly provided liquidity for the market and overwhelmed the market with TL, or it could have given the liquidity that the market needed to the banking sector. However, we should clarify a point here. If the Central Bank had offered credits to the market, the Net Domestic Assets target (-TL 1.2 quadrillion ceiling target as explained before) would have been exceeded, and this would have meant the end of the monetary program. A divergence from the target would have led to a hesitation on the reliability of the Central Bank in the international and domestic markets, and expectations on the inability of the Central Bank to meet its foreign exchange rate commitment would have emerged. The weakest link of the program was the risk of the disappearance of confidence in the Central Bank.

2.2.32   The market should have primarily known that the key risk of the program was the interest risk resulting from the very nature of the program itself. Then the market should have projected its behaviors and expectations accordingly. Furthermore, the market agents should have read between the lines that the Central Bank would not provide the market with liquidity when confronted with increasing interest rates. Before accusing the Central Bank, we should point out an "unbelievable" error committed by the market.

2.2.33   This crisis was a natural result of a series of events: the program began before making an increase in the foreign exchange rate, the BRSA which would bring the market agents (and in general the banks) under discipline began operating rather late, privatization slowed down, discussions emerged about the realization of the structural reforms. Consumption increased as a result of the credits opened by the banking system and the decline in the interest rates, and the exchange rate increase remained under the inflation rate. Therefore, the overvaluation of TL caused an uneasiness among foreign investors (assessed in general as hot money). The current account trade balance was yielding deficit and would in a short time reach the critical level of 5 percent of the GNP. According to the monetary program, the Central Bank could provide liquidity for the market on the condition that foreign currency be brought into the bank. Both the foreign capital inflow to Turkey and the sales of foreign currency by all sectors and primarily by the financial system taking short position led to an emergence of liquidity in the market and a decrease in the interest rates. What if the opposite had occurred?

2.2.34 The uneasiness on the part of foreigners about the widening current account deficit and the implementation of the program in the future might have led to the opposite situation. And it happened. Foreigners attempted to liquidate the TL and foreign currency instruments in order to buy foreign currency, and then escape from Turkey. The sales of the guarantees which had been given by the banks to the foreigners with the aim to take credits caused similar results. An amount of US $10 billion was needed to finance the balance of payments. Under these conditions, there was a substantial outflow of foreign currency from Turkey, which led naturally to a market short of TL and with high interest rates. If the Central Bank had supplied the market with liquidity, the financial sector might have calmed down. However, there was the risk that this liquidity be shifted either to expenditures – which would have led Turkey to hyper-inflation – or to foreign currency directly. In the case of a high demand for foreign currency, the reserves of the Central Bank would inevitably be melted down, and the interest rates would increase due to the decrease of liquidity in the money market.

2.2.35 After the transfer of Demirbank to the Saving Deposit Insurance Fund (on November 22) the Central Bank supplied the market with a substantial liquidity; thus, the target of the Net Domestic Revenues was met. However, as a result of the shift of this liquidity to foreign currency, the Central Bank had a substantial loss of foreign currency, and the floor target of US

$13.5 billion in the Net International Reserves was not met (for performance criteria, see "Monetary and exchange rate policies"). The Central Bank announced that the Net Domestic Assets item was frozen by 30 November, 2000. Despite high interest rates, the demand for foreign currency did not cease. An additional measures package was announced on December 6, and the IMF revised the end-December 2000 Net International Reserves floor to US $10.4 billion. The markets appeared to calm down; nevertheless, the demand for foreign currency did not cease, and continued until February. In the meantime, the Central Bank had to sell "at a low price" several billion dollars of foreign currency.

2.2.36 The main subject to be discussed at this point is the abandonment of the foreign currency peg system after the process of November. Once an uneasiness emerged in the market, in other words once the market agents believed that the Central Bank could not fulfill its foreign exchange rate commitment or that the public debts could not be managed, it became difficult to calm down the market. Several countries have experienced similar events. Once the Central Bank loses its reliability, devaluation becomes inevitable sooner or later. And it was the case. The floating exchange rate regime was adopted in February 2001. While 1 US $ was TL 679,162 and 1 Euro was TL 624,353 at the end of January 2001, 1 US $ increased to TL 906,164 and 1 Euro to TL 830,590 at the end of February.

2.2.37 After the liquidity crisis in November 2000, the IMF recommended the floating exchange rate regime. Otherwise, the international reserves would melt down against the demand for foreign currency and could not meet the demand. However, the IMF was not insistent on the floating exchange rate regime since the economy administration of the time guaranteed that additional measures would be taken and that the reforms would be carried out. Nevertheless, the economic environment was foggy. Demand was decreased in the real economy, production was rapidly declining, and unemployment increasing. Money was not circulating in the economy. While refraining from paying

Table 7. Performance Criteria of the Central Bank of Turkey and Realizations

	NDA ceiling target (in trillion TL)	NDA realized (in trillion TL)	NIR floor target (in million US $)	NIR realized (in million US $)
December 31,1999	-1,200	-1,437	12,000	16,757
March 31, 2000	-1,200	-1,260	12,000	16,657
June 30, 2000	-1,200	-1,295	12,750	17,339
September 30,2000	-1,200	-1,307	12,750	17,874
December 31, 2000	-1,200	1,060	13,500	12,488

SOURCE: CBRT

their debts, debtors were attempting to collect their credits. The devaluation of February 2001 was in fact a continuation of the November 2000 crisis. However, the foreign exchange rate increase was delayed due to high interest rates. High interest rates and slow circulation of money led to deterioration in cash flows. Almost all the sectors of society, including the Treasury, believed that the Central Bank would depreciate the TL, and the result was devaluation. That was the beginning of a new era in Turkey. Turkey had to adopt the floating exchange rate regime. However, a major part of society was not familiar at all with this implementation because the floating exchange rate regime had never been implemented in Turkey before. The assignment of Kemal Derviş was a continuation of this process. A series of measures were to be taken, primarily in the banking sector. Structural reforms were the prerequisite to carry on with the IMF. The financing of the public sector should be sustainable; otherwise, the same targets would be attained under "radical" measures.

IMPORTANT DEVELOPMENTS AFFECTING THE ECONOMY IN 2000

January 1, 2000 Stabilization program began to be implemented.

January 11, 2000 The Treasury issued US $1.5 billion bonds with a maturity of 30 years in the international capital markets.

January 21, 2000 International arbitration was accepted to work retrospectively.

January 26, 2000 The Treasury issued Euro 1 billion bonds with a maturity of 10 years in the international capital markets.

March 10, 2000 The first Letter of Intent was submitted to the IMF.

April 12, 2000 A proposal of US $2,525 million excluding VAT was given to the third GSM tender.

April 25, 2000 The international credit rating institution Standard & Poors increased the credit note of Turkey.

May 5, 2000 An immediate solvency ratio obligation was adopted for the foreign currency long position of the banks.

May 8, 2000 Primary dealership system was adopted and applications by nineteen banks were accepted.

June 1, 2000 Legislation related to the Net Foreign Currency position calculation was put into effect; the blanket guarantee was replaced by a deposit protection scheme protecting saving deposits up to TL 100 billion; it was announced that this limit would decrease to TL 50 billion in 2001.

June 22, 2000 The second Letter of Intent was submitted to the IMF.

August 31, 2000 BRSA began operation.

September 4, 2000 No proposal was given to the sale of 20 percent of Türk Telekom.

September 26, 2000 The President vetoed the decree related to the privatization of the state banks.

September 29, 2000 IMF extended to December the third portion of the credit to be given to Turkey.

October 27, 2000 BRSA announced that Etibank and Bank Kapital had been transferred to the SDIF.

November 3, 2000 BRSA announced that the Treasury would give to SDIF US \$6.1 billion government domestic debt instruments for the recovery of eight banks transferred to the Fund.

November 21, 2000 BRSA announced that the obligatory deposit fund would be decreased to 4 from 6 at the beginning of 2001.

November 22, 2000 CBT supplied TL 1,688 trillion fund to eliminate liquidity shortage in the market; however, it diverted from the Net Domestic Assets target.

November 27, 2000 CBT assisted the banks in immediate solvency.

November 29, 2000 NIR item of the CBT was realized under the floor target by end-year US \$13.5 billion.

November 30, 2000 CBT announced that the NDA item was frozen by November, and that it would stop providing liquidity to the market.

December 6, 2000 Demirbank was transferred to SDIF, and its license to conduct banking transactions was canceled.

December 6, 2000 The Prime Minister announced that Telekom and THY would be sold (partially), and the IMF announced on the same day that a total amount of US $10.4 billion financing was supplied, US $7.5 billion of it being Supplemental Reserve Facility.

December 18, 2000 The third Letter of Intent was submitted to the IMF.

SOURCE: CBT

CHAPTER III

Transition to a stronger economy program adopted after the February 2001 crisis and assessment of its results

3.1 Main features of the transition to a stronger economy program

Following the float of the Turkish Lira on February 22, 2001, a new Letter of Intent was signed with the IMF at the beginning of May. Even though the problems were more severe than those at the beginning of 2000, the objectives were similar: "disinflate the Turkish economy, strengthen the fiscal accounts, and reform the structure of the Turkish economy as a condition for setting economic growth on a sustainable basis and moving Turkey closer to its goal of joining the European Union". In support of this new program, an augmentation to the equivalent of SDR 6.3 billion was requested in the arrangement. New policies would then be adopted on a number of subjects such as the net domestic assets (NDA), the privatization of Türk Telekom, and the approval of the Electricity Market Law. The float required a recalibration of economic policies and short-term policy goals.

The economy was still under the impact of the crisis, and a severe disturbance was observed in macroeconomic balances. The economy was in a trend of negative growth, and a decrease by 3 percent in real GNP was expected. The depreciation of the Turkish Lira after the float would inevitably be reflected in inflation. The banking sector was in a difficult situation due to problems with the re-collection of credits, and to decreasing prices and liquidity of its large portfolio of government domestic debt instruments. A steady erosion of solvency and a capital inadequacy were observed in private banks. This problem was not only related to SDIF-owned banks, but to nearly all private and state banks which should be recapitalized and restructured, and whose fiscal transparency should be improved.

Financial instability caused a disturbance in the balance of the public sector, and the ratio of the public debt to the national income which had been targeted to reduce at the beginning of 2000 increased. Proper monetary and fiscal policies should be adopted in order to combat inflation, to achieve fiscal discipline, and to restructure the fiscal sector.

Therefore, a new program was introduced. This section explores the basic features, and the policy goals and implementations of the program.

GOALS OF THE PROGRAM AND NECESSARY STRATEGIES TO ACHIEVE THESE GOALS

GOALS:

a. to minimize uncertainty and instability.

b. to establish new and contemporary corporate structures.

c. to adopt structural policies for a stronger economy.

d. to adopt macroeconomic policies aimed at financial stability and growth.

e. to achieve a sustainable economic growth.

f. to establish a fair income distribution among all segments of the population and regions of the country.

STRATEGIES TO BE ADOPTED TO ACHIEVE THESE GOALS

a. restructuring of the banking system.

b. restructuring of the borrowing system.

c. transition to the implementation of inflation targeting in the monetary policy within the framework of the floating exchange rate regime.

d. wage and price decisions in line with the inflation target.

e. improving the economic environment through enhanced transparency, better governance, and a strengthened regulatory environment.

f. finding support from the World Bank

3.1.1 STRUCTURAL REFORM AND LEGAL ARRANGEMENTS

a) Restructuring of the Fiscal Sector

Legal arrangements related to the banking sector and the Central Bank should be carried out within this framework. State banks would work in an efficient way, and would not engage in unsound practices leading to duty losses; the independent governing board of the state banks would also formulate plans for the privatization of these banks; the process of transferring the insolvent bank Emlak to Ziraat would continue; SDIF banks would be merged under the names of a few banks; the medium-sized Demirbank would be sold in a short term; arrangements would be made for capital strengthening of private banks.

- Capital strengthening plans should be carried out by the banks to achieve stable fiscal markets and real sector. To this end, the Banking Law would be amended in several respects.

- The full guarantee protecting deposits and other liabilities of the banks would continue.

- The increasing funding needs to cover cash deficits had forced the state- and SDIF-owned banks into large-scale overnight funding, which had led to a disturbance in both the market equilibrium and the financial structures of the banks themselves. For this reason, government papers bearing below-market yields instruments in the portfolio of the state-owned banks would be replaced with government securities at market terms; remaining duty losses would thus be eliminated. Within a certain program, these securities would be sold directly or through repurchase agreements to the Central Bank, and the state- and SDIF-owned banks could then use that liquidity to eliminate the overnight borrowing from commercial banks and other market sources. The resultant excess liquidity in the financial system would be absorbed by the Central Bank through inverse repo and interbank transactions. As observed in the following table, in 2001 the Treasury offered a large amount of government domestic debt instruments to state- and SDIF-owned banks with the aim to strengthen their financial structures. These securities would then be sold directly or through repurchase agreements to the Central Bank. As a result, state and SDIF banks would meet their liabilities.The monetary growth based on the increase in the Net Domestic Assets would in turn affect the new equilibrium level of the foreign exchange rate, inflation, and interest rates.

Table 8. Sources Transferred to State and SDIF Banks

	in trillion TL	Share in GDP (%)
1. State Banks	28,858	15.8
Duty Losses by end-2000	17,279	9.5
Increase in Duty Losses in 2001	7,759	4.3
Capital Support in 2001	3,550	2.0
2. Instruments exported to SDIF by Treasury	21,581	11.9

SOURCE: BRSA

b) Enhancing Transparency in the Public Sector and Strengthening of the Public Financing

- The most important arrangement within this framework was the law to be submitted to parliament on public finance and debt management, aiming at enhancing the transparency and accountability of fiscal management. This law would define clear borrowing rules and limits for the public sector, and incorporate into the budget the on-lending and debt guarantee operations of the treasury, thus expanding the cover to include both the domestic and external borrowings and state guaranteed debt system – which had been regulated before with various legal texts. Furthermore, a flexible, efficient and speedy collection and management of debt would take place. A debt management report would be submitted to parliament every three months, giving the details on the debt collected and guarantees provided.

- Public Tender Law would be revised with the aim to establish a more competitive and efficient system in line with international standards. With this law, the turnkey tender which was based on the application project would be made, leading to a more efficient and competitive tender method and preventing an increase in the costs of projects to be put out to tender.

  - In addition to forty-six budgetary funds and six extra-budgetary funds (EBFs) already closed, the fifteen remaining budgetary funds and two EBFs would be closed with the aim to achieve an ultimate consolidation in the funding system and thus to improve budget control and transparency.

  - Expropriation Law would be revised as well. The principle that the amount should be paid in cash and in advance as anticipated in the Constitution and Law was abused in practice. Administrations were not acting in conformity with fiscal discipline in the expropriation decision and valuation. According to the new law, expropriation could not take place before making the necessary allocation. Purchase and barter would be first applied. In the case of a disagreement, the expropriation value would be set by the court.

c) Enhancing Competition and Efficiency in the Economy

Legal arrangements affecting a large part of society were put on the agenda with the aim to enhance competition and efficiency.

- **The law to reform the sugar market:** The aim was to achieve stability in the market by establishing procedures and principles regulating sugar beet production, pricing, and marketing. Beginning from the period 2002–2003, the government would not annouce any price. The sugar beet market would be managed by a committee who would prevent an excess production, thus a loss in the public budget. The producer would decide according to the price, whether to sow sugar beet or not before the seed time. With the introduction of direct income support for farmers, their decreasing revenues would be prevented. Sugar factories would be privatized.

- **The tobacco law:** Procedures and principles regulating the pricing, distribution, sales and control of tobacco and alcoholic beverages would be established by the Tobacco and Alcoholic Beverages Market Regulating Committee. Beginning from the production period of 2002, there would not be any purchase on behalf and account of the government, and the necessary infrastructure for the privatization of production and marketing departments of TEKEL (tobacco and alcoholic beverages company) would be established. Tobacco in excess would no longer be left to rot or to be burnt. Uncertainty on the part of the producer would be eliminated by means of contracts and bidding, and the tobacco producer would be supported by an alternative product project and direct income support.

- **Natural gas law:** This legislation included a framework for liberalization of the natural gas market leading to a high quality, continuous, cheap, competitive and environment-friendly gas supply to consumers. According to the new law, the monopoly of BOTAŞ (the natural gas company) in the import, transmission, and distribution of gas would be replaced by private sector participation. The market would thus be improved in terms of financial strength, stability, and transparency. The natural gas market would be included in the electricity market committee, and managed by an independent administration.

- **Privatization of Türk Telekom:** With the aim to speed up the privatization of Türk Telekom, the government intended to adopt legislation to authorize divestiture of up to a hundred percent of Türk Telekom, excluding a golden share which would remain with the government (the golden share covering security and protection of national interests); to reserve five percent of the shares of Türk Telekom for employees and small investors; to remove the monopoly of Türk Telekom on fixed lines; to transfer all licensing authority for telecommunication services and infrastructure to the Telecommunication Regulatory Authority; to appoint the members of the new professional board and management team who would improve the terms at which Türk Telekom would be privatized; and to allow foreign ownership of the shares of Türk Telekom below fifty percent.

- **Civil aviation law:** Parliament has passed a law liberalizing domestic airline fares, allowing Turkish Airlines and other airlines companies to fix their price tariffs and to utilize the existing aeroplane capacities in an efficient way by differentiating prices according to certain days and hours. Furthermore, this arrangement which would enhance competition in the sector could increase employment in the medium- and long-term. The development of the sector would be beneficial for tourism. Funding of this sector would be encouraged, considering both Turkish residents and Turkish citizens living abroad.

d) Enhancing Social Dialogue

- **Job security law:** This law was placed within the short-term priorities in the EU National Program, and negotiations for the draft law began between the representatives of the employers and trade unions, and with their joint commission.

- **The law on the economic and social council:** The aim was to establish an intensive dialogue with the employers and trade unions. To this end, following the adoption of the Law on the Economic and Social Council, the Council would be in a position to hold frequent and regular meetings, to assess economic developments, and to initiate social dialogue.

e) Real Economy Measures:

- Additional measures were projected to be taken to increase export, and within this framework:
- Credit opportunities of Eximbank would be increased within the framework of financing provided by the budget and other sources.
- VAT payments would be speeded up in exports.
- Bureaucratic procedures would be minimized in support lending.

- A law fully implementing the constitutional amendment on international arbitration would be passed with the aim to speed up the direct inflow of foreign capital in Turkey. In addition, an action plan had been made to remove the administrative and bureaucratic obstacles to direct investment.

- With the aim to minimize the negative effect of the crisis on tradesmen, artisans, small- and medium-sized enterprises, and the agricultural sector, an allowance of TL 400 trillion was granted to the budget in order to limit the costs which would be reflected on the interests from the credits they had taken from Ziraat and Halk banks.

3.1.2   MACROECONOMIC TARGETS

The crises of November 2000 and February 2001 had had a destructive impact on all sectors, primarily on the banking sector, and imposed a heavy burden on public finances. As a result of the increase in the interest rates and transition to the floating exchange rate regime, an uncertainty about foreign exchange rates emerged, shaking economic units' confidence in the future, causing a negative effect on the economy, and leading to a contraction in the economy and to a sharp increase in unemployment. With the depreciation of TL, a leap was observed in inflation.

According to the economy administration of the time, the increase in the exchange rates had caused an increase in the competitive power of Turkey, and this increasing competitive power was the way out for Turkey. Due to the depreciation of TL, there was indeed an increase in the competitive power of Turkey; however, a lot of burden, primarily increased interest rates, carried on affecting production costs negatively. Therefore, after a decline in the first half of 2001, growth was expected to resume in the second half of the year. Nevertheless, real GNP was expected to fall by 3 percent in 2001 (as seen in the following table). On the other hand, the inevitable effect of the increase in foreign exchange rates on prices was reflected on the 2001 targets. In 2001, an increase by 49.4 percent was expected in the deflator (the increase due to prices in the Nominal National Income increase); an increase by 57.6 percent was expected in WPI, and an increase by 52.5 percent in CPI. The economy was expected to revive from the beginning of 2002, and the inflation rates would decline gradually.

Table 9. Macroeconomic Targets

	1999	2000	2001P	2002P	2003P
Growth	-6.1	6.1	-3.0	5.0	6.0
Deflator	55.8	51.6	49.4	28.3	16.5
WPI (end-year)	62.9	32.7	57.6	16.6	12.4
CPI (end-year)	68.8	39.0	52.5	20.0	15.0

THE FISCAL POLICY IN THE TRANSITION TO A STRONGER ECONOMY

At the beginning of the stabilization program of 2000, one of the goals was to combat high inflation – of which the main cause was considered to be high public deficits – and the other to reduce the ratio of the rapidly increasing public deficit to the national income, and to achieve sustainable debt management. Hence, as mentioned before, reducing public deficits, increasing public primary surplus, minimizing public borrowing, and decreasing real interest rates were mainly focused on.

Besides high public deficits, the net external debt paying position of the public sector after 1994 created pressure on vulnerable domestic fiscal markets, leading to sustainable high interest rates. During that period, high real interest rates had stemmed from a high and variable inflationist environment, leading to an increase in risk premium. Between 1992 and 1999, the annual average GNP growth rate had realized below four percent, and the domestic debt real interest rate 32 percent. High real interest rates had further widened the borrowing need of the public sector, leading Turkey to a debt-interest rate vicious circle. The increase in the debt stock caused worries about the sustainability of the situation.

However, the failure of the 2000 program gave rise to further worries about the public deficit and public debt. The transition to a stronger economy program would then primarily focus on debt management. Thus, this goal would be emphasized in fiscal policy implementations.

Table 10. Consolidated budget Developments and the Target of 2001

CONSOLIDATED BUDGET	GNP %		
	1999	2000	2001
REVENUES	23.9	25.9	25.5
Tax Revenues	18.9	21.0	20.5
- Direct Taxes	8.6	8.6	7.3
- Indirect Taxes	10.3	12.4	13.3
Non-Tax Revenues	5.0	4.8	5.0
NON-INTEREST EXPENDITURES	21.8	20.5	19.7
Personnel Expenditure	8.8	7.9	7.8
Other Current	2.8	2.8	2.6
Investment	1.8	1.8	2.1
Transfers	8.4	7.9	7.4
-Transfer to SEEs	0.7	0.9	0.5
-Interest Differential Payment to State Banks	0.0	0.1	0.2
-Agricultural Subsidies	0.3	0.3	0.6
-Transfer to Funds	1.3	1.6	0.5
-Social Security Institutions	3.5	2.6	2.8
-Tax Rebates to Pensioners	1.5	1.3	1.1
-Others	1.1	1.1	1.6
PRIMARY BALANCE	2.1	5.4	5.6
PRIMARY BALANCE	1.5	4.6	5.1
(excl. privatization, interest revenue and CBT profit)			

SOURCE: TT

Graph 9. Course of the Ratio of Primary Surplus/GNP and the Target of 2001 and 2002 (%)

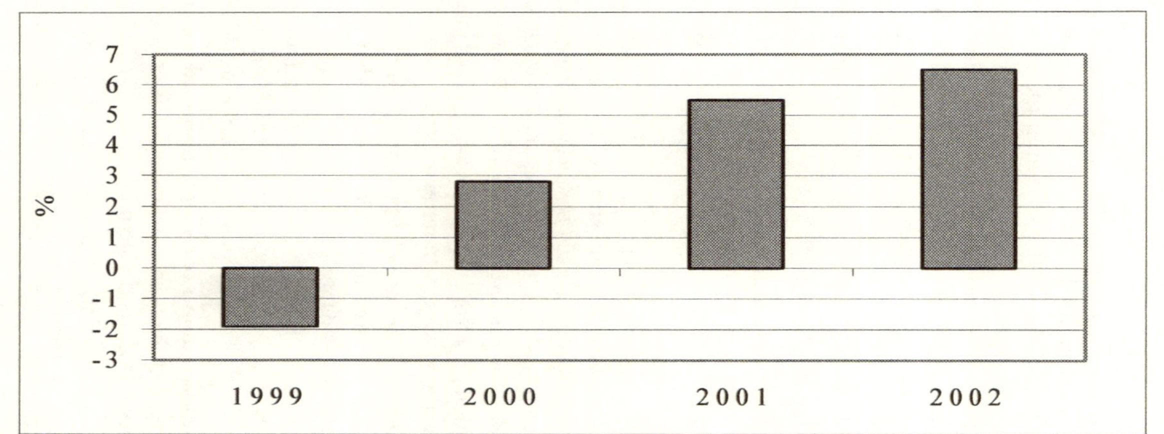

SOURCE: TT

The ratio of the total primary surplus of the public sector to the GNP which had realized 3 percent in 2000 was projected to increase to 5.5 percent in 2001, and to 6.5 percent in 2002 and 2003. Within this framework, the increase to 5.1 percent in 2001 from 4.6 percent in 2000 of the ratio of the consolidated budget primary surplus to the GNP (as seen in the above table), and the decrease to 0.4 percent in 2001 from 1.8 percent in 2000 of the primary deficit of the public sector (including SEEs and other public institutions) were defined as critical indications of the implementation of the program.

EXPENDITURE-LIMITING MEASURES IN THE TRANSITION TO A STRONGER ECONOMY PROGRAM

i   The nominal increase in the non-interest expenditures was to be kept below the nominal increase of the GNP. Thus, a real decrease by 9 percent was targeted in the expenditures of 2000 in 2001.

ii   Public sector expenditures would be taken under control, leading to maximum savings. To this end, Public Sector Savings Circular should be strictly implemented. The Finance Ministry could impose blockage on certain allowance items.

iii   Some 1½ percentage points of GNP would be saved by adjusting current expenditure, transfers, and investment by less than the revision in the inflation target.

iv   In addition, savings of 0.3 percent of GNP would be generated during the implementation of the budget by cuts in other current expenditure.

v   0.2 percent of the GNP was allocated to finance the payments of the state banks resulting from the differences in the interest rates. Liabilities exceeding the allocation would not be accepted.

vi   The total number of civil servants would not increase in 2001 in spite of the need to raise employment in key social sectors (mostly health and education).

vii   Individual demands for wage and salary increases would not be taken into consideration.

viii   New investment projects would not be proposed, except emergency projects. Multiyear tenders would not be made.

ix   Proposals necessitating an increase in the expenditures, including an expansion in the organization or new personnel employment, would not be put on the agenda.

x   Necessary arrangements would be made to increase the efficiency of SEEs. The number of personnel would not increase, overtime payments would be strictly limited, current expenditures would be controlled, and investment expenditures would be rationalized.

xi   Support price increases would be kept at targeted inflation, and the volume of support would be limited according to the financing opportunities of the institutions.

xii   Health expenditures of the social security institutions would be put under discipline.

xiii   Vehicle use would be limited in the public sector, and the Vehicle Law would be strictly implemented.

REVENUE INCREASING ARRANGEMENTS

i   Measures taken at the end of 2000 to increase tax revenues would continue to be implemented.

ii   Automatic pricing mechanism would carry on in fuel, Fuel Consumption Tax would be kept at least at the targeted inflation rate, and the collection of Fuel Consumption Tax would have a share of 2.8 percent in the GNP.

iii   Prices of the products based on imports, particularly from the energy and petrolium sectors, would be immediately adjusted according to changing exchange rates, increasing costs, and economic realities.

iv   In order to strengthen the tax base, the use of a tax identification number would be gradually extended.

v   By means of tax inspections, tax evasion would be reduced.

vi   With the aim to increase tax collection, delinquent tax due was increased in accordance with inflation rate.

vii   Direct purchases of government securities by individuals would be encouraged through amendments in the structure of the taxation of financial instruments.

Table 11. Foreign Exchange Rate Regimes and Monetary Policies

INDICATIVE CEILINGS FOR BASE MONEY*

2001	CEILINGS (IN TRILLION TL)
May 31	5,900
July 30	6,050
August 31	6,300 (7,125)
October 31	6,800 (7,550)
December 31	7,300 (7,750)

*Base money is defined as currency issued by the CBT, plus the banking sector's obligatory reserve, plus the banking sector's free deposits in Turkish lira with the CBT

Figures in parentheses are revised figures in July 31, 2001.

1.1 The growth level of base money would be kept broadly in line with the indicative ceiling set for Net Domestic Assets (NDA) excluding net sources allocated for the Treasury's financing needs.

1.2 Base money was projected to grow in 2001 by 25.8 percent, or by 47 percent after adjusting for the end-2000 Bayram and the cut in the reserve requirement coefficient in early 2001.

1.3 Changes in the interest and inflation rates were considered as the necessary causes to revise the growth in the base money.

CEILINGS FOR NET DOMESTIC ASSETS[*]

2001	CEILINGS (IN TRILLION TL)
May 31 (performance criterion)	9,750
June 30 (performance criterion)	13,250
August 31 (performance criterion)	15,850 (17,250)
October 30 (performance criterion)	19,500 (21,150)
December 31 (indicative ceiling)	21,000 (22,400)

*NDA = (Net) Cash credits to public sector (incl. Public Debt Management Support Account) (+, -), Fund Account (-), Deposits of Non-Bank Sector (-), Cash credits to banking sector (+), Open Market Operations (+, -), Valuation account (+,-), IMF emergency assistance account (+), Other items (+, -), Foreign currency stocks supplied by the parliament (+)

Figures in parentheses are revised figures in July 31, 2001.

2.1 NDA variable would be increased in parallel with the foreign currency stock supplied by the parliament and the additional financing for treasury debt management support.

2.2 Thus the NDA ceiling was limited with the credits to be supplied to the market and public sector.

FLOORS FOR NET INTERNATIONAL RESERVES[*] BEING A SUB-ITEM OF NET EXTERNAL ASSETS OF THE PARLIAMENT

2001	FLOORS ON CHANGE IN NIR DURING THE SPECIFIED PERIODS (IN MILLION US $)
May (performance criterion)	-1,500
June (performance criterion)	-2,900
July–Aug. (performance criterion)	-2,000
Sept.–Nov. (performance criterion)	-2,600
Nov.–Dec. (indicative floor)	-600

*NIR = Gross foreign assets (+), Gross international reserve liabilities (-), Net forward position of the central bank (+, -)

3.1 The limits on the changes in NIR were specified in the above table.

3.2 The limits on the changes in NIR would be increased by either the unused portion of the limit on the change in NIR from the previous period or by 25 percent of the limit during the current period, whichever is less.

TRANSITION TO A STRONGER ECONOMY AND EXTERNAL
FINANCING

A distinguishing feature of the transition to a stronger economy
program was the external financing supplied by the IMF and
World Bank. Even though a primary surplus of US $10 billion
was targeted in the budget, it was rather difficult to finance a
deficit reaching a very high level of 15.1 percent of the GNP. The
domestic debt stock estimated to reach TL 105 quadrillion in 2001
(it was TL 36 quadrillion in 2000) and the domestic debt service
(the capital, plus its interest) of TL 78 quadrillion made the cost
of public sector financing, that is, the borrowing costs higher.
Moreover, there were external debts and payments. To supply the
domestic and external services only from domestic markets would
not be consistent with the macroeconomic expectations. For this
reason, additional external financing should be found.
Negotiations were being conducted on this subject, and the IMF
came to help because a radical approach was out of the question.
Debts were to be managed with new debts, and this time with
external debts.

The depreciation of TL would have a positive impact on
exports, but a negative one on imports. Consequently, the foreign
trade deficit would decrease. In parallel with this, an
improvement was expected in the current account trade balance
demonstrating the inflowing and outflowing foreign currency
balance due to goods and service exchanges. *In addition to the
improvement in the current account balance, external financing support was
indispensable for the success of the program. An amount of US $15.7
billion was expected from the IMF and World Bank in the January-
December period. A gross amount of US $3.7 billion, that is, a net amount
of US $2.4 billion of the portion supplied by the IMF would be transferred
to the Central Bank as reserve support. Thus, with this support for (debt
for) the Treasury, the pressure on domestic fiscal markets would be relieved.*

TRANSITION TO A STRONGER ECONOMY AND INCOMES
POLICY

An important feature of the program was the adoption of an
incomes policy in line with a targeted inflation rate. Wage

increases in the public sector would be consistent with inflation, and the disparity between civil servants and government workers which had resulted from the very large increases accorded to public sector workers by the collective agreement for the period 1999–2000 would be reduced. The sacrifice made by the population would reduce the crisis costs in terms of growth and employment, and speed up the access to growth in the second quarter of the year. Likewise, with the aim to strengthen farmers with low incomes, a direct income support system would be introduced, and support price increases in 2001 would be kept at most at targeted inflation, considering financing opportunities of the institutions. In this way, it was made clear that support for the program would be derived from those with fixed incomes, and farmers.

3.2 End of the transition to a stronger economy program, September 11 attacks, and a new three-year program in 2002

Turkey experienced crises during the years 2000 and 2001 despite the supervision of the IMF. After the failure of the crawling peg system adopted in 2000, a floating currency regime was introduced. Implementations under the transition to a stronger economy program did not aim to solve the problem; they only postponed negative results. There were attempts to overcome the liquidity crisis in markets with monetary support, and a decline in the interest rates was observed as a result of the funding of state banks by the Central Bank. However, public sector debt stock further increased due to the portfolio of government domestic debt instruments transferred to state banks to compensate duty losses, and to government domestic debt instruments transferred to the said banks as a result of banking operations. Interest burden became a large portion of the budget. We may even say that taxes were collected to pay the interests.

The fiscal system's capital was melted to a great extent due to increasing foreign currency and high interest rates. There were serious problems with capital adequacy. In a period where radical decisions could not be taken, it was attempted to overcome the liquidity crisis with the liqudity supplied to the market by the Central Bank through the purchase of Treasury debt instruments. Arrangements related to monetary policy helped to handle the crisis to a certain extent; however, they were not sufficient to solve the problems radically. There were problems concerning the implementation of structural reforms; furthermore, necessary steps towards radical changes in the budget could not be taken. Budgetary practices based on government debt rollover did not differ from those in the previous years. The outcome was failure indeed; however, there was an attempt to find pretexts for this failure. The September 11 attacks were one of them. It was obvious that macroeconomic balances could not have been established despite the substantial credit offered by the IMF. The public sector balance was alarming to a considerable degree. The ratio of the budget deficit to the national income had exceeded 15 percent, and the ratio of the public sector debt to the national income was over 90 percent. The Letter of Intent dated January 28, 2002 to the IMF pointed out to what extent Turkey had proceeded to solve her problems; and the September 11 attacks were used as a pretext for the failure.

> From the outset, Turkey's economic reform program has had two main goals: conquering the chronic and persistent high inflation of the 1990s, and overcoming the associated macroeconomic instability which has constrained our economic growth. Although the original three-year program initiated in December 1999 has had to be adapted and strengthened in the light of events, including the February 2001 crisis, we have made considerable progress. We have implemented a major fiscal adjustment to help bring about debt sustainability. We have reformed the banking sector through an operational and financial restructuring of public banks, and a strengthening of the regulation and supervision of private banks. We have also pursued disinflation both under the original crawling peg regime and following the float in February 2001. Finally, we have deepened the role of the private sector in the economy, including through reforms to facilitate privatization.

Our revised program, adopted in May 2001, was beginning to achieve its aim of restoring investor confidence in the wake of the two crises, when the events of September 11 hit. From early August onward, as confidence began to return, interest rates started to fall, and the Turkish lira stabilized. The events of September 11, however, hit Turkey particularly hard, given our debt situation and our location. This severe external shock is affecting the Turkish economy through several channels: weaker demand in industrial countries, lower tourism receipts, reduced access to international financial markets, and poorer privatization and foreign direct investment prospects. This has resulted in a projected external financing gap of US $10 billion in 2002, and weaker short-term economic growth prospects.

We have responded to the fallout of September 11 and Turkey's ongoing economic problems by deepening and extending our economic program, building on our earlier reforms. The Turkish economy is entering 2002 with greater strength thanks to the reforms carried out so far, [*but is still facing very important challenges. Chief among them is the reduction of inflation to the targeted 35 percent, the resumption of growth which should continue to be export led, and the more rapid extension of the benefits of growth to the lower-income groups.*] We are determined to build on the positive results that have emerged at the end of 2001 thanks to the success of our fiscal policies, the competitive exchange rate, and the enactment of many important structural reforms. [*Despite the progress made, Turkey continues to face difficult macroeconomic and structural policy challenges, including a substantial public debt burden, high inflation, banking sector difficulties, and extensive state involvement in the economy. To tackle these problems, while addressing the repercussions of September 11, we have decided to adopt a strengthened medium-term economic program.*]

This letter lays out in detail our economic program for 2002–04, and requests a new stand-by arrangement in its support. Based on our balance of payments needs, and our strengthened policies described below, we request the approval of a new stand-by arrangement in an amount equivalent to SDR 12,821.2 million for the period January 2002 through December 2004. The current stand-by arrangement (2000–02) will be cancelled upon approval of the new arrangement.] We will use the equivalent of SDR 4,916.4 million of what becomes available upon approval to repay outstanding resources under the Supplemental Reserve Facility.

(TURKEY, LETTER OF INTENT DATED JANUARY 28, 2002, WWW.IMF.ORG.)

The new letter of intent emphasized particularly that there still existed very important challenges, and that inflation should be reduced, the resumption of growth should continue to be export led, and the benefits of growth should be extended to the lower-income groups.

Were these basic objectives attained? What should have been done to attain them? In order to explore whether these objectives were realized or not, let us outline the new program:

3.3 Overview of the targets, strategies, and Policies in the letter of intent submitted to the IMF at the beginning of 2002

A   STRATEGIES AND OBJECTIVES FOR THE PERIOD BETWEEN 2002 AND 2004

- Our program aims to insure the economy against future crises and lay the basis for sustained noninflationary growth. First, the program will improve the economy's resilience to shocks and reduce its vulnerability to future economic crises, by (i) maintaining the exchange rate float and using inflation targeting to deliver a significant reduction in inflation, (ii) pressing ahead with bank restructuring, and (iii) ensuring a viable government debt position. Second, the program will involve fundamental structural reforms aimed at raising Turkey's growth potential. Achieving these objectives will also help move Turkey closer to the goal of EU membership.

- For 2002, our priority will be to restore financial and macroeconomic stability, and to further progress in structural reforms. To this end, we will ensure that our ambitious public sector primary surplus target of 6½ percent of GNP will be met. This, together with our active and flexible debt management strategy, should ease government debt rollover. We are also determined to deepen our structural reforms to build on the important results achieved so far. While in 2001 the sharp devaluation after the float of the Turkish lira in February and the September 11 shock raised CPI inflation to 68.5 percent, in 2002 monetary policy will be consistent with our 35 percent inflation target. Although real GNP is estimated to have declined by 8½ percent in 2001, a moderate economic recovery started in the third quarter, and is expected to continue in 2002. In light of the negative impact of the recent events on exports and tourism and our commitment to disinflation, we project real GNP growth in 2002 conservatively at 3 percent. We believe, however, that this projection has upside potential. As regards the external current account, we expect the September 11 shock, the economic recovery, and a modest rebound in the real exchange rate to result in a deficit of about US $2 billion in 2002, following an estimated surplus of a similar size in 2001.

- For 2003–04 and beyond, our key objectives are sustainable growth, together with continued disinflation and a viable debt position. Continued implementation of prudent financial policies and structural reforms will lay the basis for higher growth of at least 5 percent annually in 2003 and beyond. The move to an inflation targeting framework will underpin our disinflation efforts. Recovery in world demand and the impact of structural reform on the competitiveness of our economy will support the current account. In this context, we expect government debt to show a marked declining trend relative to GNP, and the external current account position to be fully financed, with foreign exchange reserves at safe levels.

- The role of the private sector would be enhanced in the economy *"by accelerating privatization, facilitating corporate debt restructuring, improving the business climate (including through the creation of an Investor Council), and encouraging foreign direct and domestic investment. By the end of the program period, we expect all large state economic enterprises (SEEs) to have been restructured, and most of them privatized."*

- Public sector reform would be completed. This reform *"aimed at a lasting improvement in public resource management and efficiency. Our main focus in this area will be on reforming the civil service, further consolidating the fiscal accounts, and improving fiscal reporting and transparency."*

B   PUBLIC DEBT MANAGEMENT

- In the last few months, the Treasury has been able to lengthen the maturity of domestic debt issuance and widen the range of investor participation, notwithstanding the turbulent conditions in world markets. We lengthened the average maturity of Treasury bill issuance to nearly 6 months in November, the longest since May, which illustrates growing market confidence. Retail investors augmented their securities holdings, spurred by the recent increase in the tax exemption threshold and improving domestic market conditions. With demand from insurance companies and foreign investors also on the rise, this diversified the investor base. Meanwhile, the Treasury issued US $1.5 billion in international bonds during the final quarter of the year, exceeding expectations under difficult international market conditions.

- For 2002, we expect that additional external financing and the strong financial position of state banks will limit the domestic borrowing needs from the private sector to comfortable levels, facilitating a smooth rollover of the government's domestic debt. (...) Beyond this, we will take several new debt management initiatives in 2002 to improve the robustness of the debt program to periods of market weakness, reduce remaining market concerns about the rollover, and diversify the investor base. In Treasury bill auctions and public offerings, we will continue to lengthen average maturity to the extent demand allows and to encourage a diverse range of investors. This should further reduce the gross borrowing requirement from the market, and hence the private banks' rollover ratio. We will also provide instruments and a market structure which seek to ensure that banks continue to play a major role in the funding of government debt. Accordingly, in issuing new domestic debt we will pay particular attention to the need to allow banks to match their foreign exchange and interest rate exposures.

- In January 2002, we will resume the program of Floating Rate Note (FRN) auctions which had halted in November 2000. By further increasing the maturity of the Treasury's debt, this program will allow a reduction in the Treasury's gross borrowing requirement, while providing an instrument which meets banks' needs concerning interest rate risk and liquidity.

- To further enhance the liquidity of domestic debt, we will reintroduce a primary dealer program by end-September 2002 (structural benchmark).

- Liquidity in the government securities market will be helped by liquidity in other financial instrument markets. Therefore, the deepening of the interbank money market and creation of a Turkish Interbank Offer Rate described in paragraph 25 will be helpful for debt management.

- We will continue to issue, subject to market conditions, domestic fx-denominated and fx-indexed bonds, as well as international bonds, to further lower the gross domestic borrowing requirement while maintaining a diverse investor base and mix of instruments.

C MONETARY POLICY

- The main goal of monetary policy will be to reduce inflation to 35 percent by end-2002.

- In May 2001, we took the first crucial step toward inflation targeting, by granting the CBT full operational independence to pursue the goal of price stability.

- We are taking important steps to fulfill the remaining conditions for the successful launch of inflation targeting. First, we have sustained our efforts to raise the public sector primary surplus and to improve debt management. This has put the public finances in significantly better shape which, in time, will give monetary policy greater freedom to reduce inflation. Second, we will continue to strengthen the banking system which, as a side benefit, will considerably ease the pressures facing monetary policy. Third, we believe that our strengthened economic program will sustain the recent improvement in financial market conditions, increased confidence in the Turkish lira, and exchange rate stability. Together with our adherence to the program's money supply targets, monthly inflation should soon fall quite sharply and, with it, expectations of inflation for the remainder of the year. Fourth, we will continue our technical preparations for the introduction of inflation targeting (...). We believe that these four steps will play an important role in meeting all of the pre-conditions for successful inflation targeting by mid-year.

- In support of the early introduction of inflation targeting, we are strengthening incomes policy and taking steps to reduce backward indexation in the economy.

- We will maintain the floating exchange rate regime,

which is central to our monetary policy and the sustained reduction of inflation.

- We are also introducing reforms to improve the working of the money and foreign exchange markets:

    - Developing the money market. (…)

    - Developing forward and futures markets. (…)

    - Currency transactions of state economic enterprises. Consistent with the change to floating exchange rates, in January 2002 the Privatization Agency will authorize companies in its portfolio to transact their foreign exchange business not at the CBT official rate, but at the market rate. The oil and gas companies (TÜPRAŞ and BOTAŞ) will work with state banks to improve their foreign exchange practices, to minimize lumpy transactions in the foreign exchange market. In this connection, the Treasury has already issued BOTAŞ this instruction, and has ended the practice of requiring this company to seek market quotations (and, in so doing, revealing its foreign exchange needs) from major market participants.

    - Implementation of the monetary program will be monitored through performance criteria on the monetary base and net international reserves (NIR), and indicative limits on net domestic assets (NDA).

D BANKING REFORM

- The program aims to continue the strengthening of the banking system and oversight framework that has been underway since 1999.

- In 2001 we completed the financial restructuring of state banks, and for 2002 our objective is to conclude their operational restructuring.

- We are introducing a comprehensive plan to further strengthen the private banking system so that it can perform its crucial role of financial intermediation to the real sector.

- The rigorous evaluation of banks' loan portfolios is an essential element of the new support scheme, providing a clear basis for investors and the government to inject necessary new capital into the banking system. In January 2002, the BRSA will issue guidelines to be applied in the evaluation, including the use of uniform criteria (prior action). The targeted evaluation of loan portfolios, collaterals, and certain other exposures will be performed by banks' existing external auditors, and will be completed by end-March 2002. Third-party auditing firms will be appointed by the BRSA by end-March 2002 to verify that the guidelines have been followed, and to ensure the integrity of the process (structural benchmark). The BRSA will complete the final interpretation of the evaluations by end-April 2002, and by May 15, 2002 will send letters to banks stipulating required actions on the basis of this interpretation (the latter is a prior action for the second review). Any losses identified in the evaluation will be fully absorbed by writing down existing shares. The evaluation results will be incorporated into banks' end-June 2002 financial statements.

- Public capital support will be provided to solvent private banks whose owners are prepared to raise equity to certain thresholds.

- We remain committed to the speedy resolution of banks taken over by the SDIF.

- We will take a number of measures to further strengthen the legal and regulatory framework:

    - Laws and regulations regarding loan classification, loan loss provisioning, and collateral valuation will be amended as necessary following the portfolio reviews by end-June 2002. As a first step, we will pass as a prior action a legal amendment in January 2002 to eliminate with immediate effect the existing four-year transition rule for loan loss provisioning.

- As of January 1, 2002, two important regulations became effective: including in CAR calculations capital charges for market risks on a solo basis; and monitoring of internal control and risk management systems. Moreover, trial implementation of a new accounting system in line with International Accounting Standards (IAS) will begin in January 2002 (prior action). The inclusion of off-balance sheet repos in banks' balance sheets was announced in December 2001, and will take effect as of February 1, 2002. Effective July 1, 2002, capital charges for market risks will be included on a consolidated basis when calculating the CAR. Moreover, following the trial implementation the BRSA will evaluate the experience and issue by end-June 2002 a revised regulation on the new accounting standards to ensure that banks' end-2002 balance sheets comply with IAS (structural performance criterion for end-June 2002).

E CORPORATE DEBT RESTRUCTURING

- We are strengthening the framework for corporate debt restructuring to complement the restructuring of the banking sector. The existing legal, judicial, and institutional frameworks are inadequate for the scale of restructuring that is needed. As a first step, in January 2002 we will introduce a voluntary market-based framework (the "Istanbul Approach") for dealing case-by-case with multicreditor exposures to large and medium-size borrowers.

- To facilitate corporate debt restructuring, we are also

110

undertaking a major review of the bankruptcy and foreclosure frameworks, which will be overhauled as needed. This will complement our ongoing work of modernizing our Civil and Commercial Codes to conform with EU rules and directives.

- Financial disclosure of companies and especially of large corporate groups will be improved, and corporate governance standards strengthened. The Capital Markets Board (CMB) will introduce international accounting standards, including inflation accounting provisions, by January 1, 2003. Starting end-March 2002, the CMB will require corporate groups to provide consolidated financial statements, and will set up a dedicated group to monitor their finances. As of the same date, the CMB will also require corporate groups with financial affiliates to provide consolidated group statements and share those statements with the BRSA.

F   PUBLIC SECTOR REFORM

- We will significantly strengthen the central government's underlying fiscal position by implementing our ambitious public sector reform program. In particular, we will aim to increase expenditure efficiency (allowing more to be done with less), and reform the tax system (to broaden the base and make it more sustainable), and the civil service (to increase efficiency and improve the quality of the public service). To alleviate the impacts of these actions on the most vulnerable members of society, we will enhance and better target our social spending.

- Our key reform initiatives for the central government include the following:
    - To strengthen expenditure efficiency, we will improve procurement methods and rationalize the public investment program. The Public Procurement Law in line with UN standards

(UNCITRAL) was adopted by parliament on January 4, 2002. Following its adoption, we will immediately begin the work necessary to allow it to take effect by January 1, 2003, including establishing an independent procurement agency by end-March 2002 (structural benchmark), and changing laws and regulations to make them consistent with the new framework. To further improve the transparency and competitiveness of public procurement, we expect parliament to amend the Public Procurement Law by end-May 2002, to (i) bring the real value of the thresholds toward those in line with international best practice and (ii) extend the minimum time period for procurement applicable for cases below the thresholds. Public investment has already been rationalized in the 2002 fiscal framework, with 353 (of 5,047) main projects and 649 sub-projects removed from the roster, and a 20 percent reduction in both total costs and the estimated time to completion. Building on this, we will compile a comprehensive list of projects to be phased out in time to make decisions for the 2003 budget.

-   We will specify an ambitious three-year plan to reform the tax system, which the Council of Ministers will approve in January 2002 (prior action). The plan will establish two phases of tax reform to be implemented in 2002. The first phase, to be enacted in a revenue-neutral manner by end-April 2002 (structural benchmark), will focus on simplifying the system of indirect taxation and lessening distortions associated with the taxation of nominal interest income. The second phase will deal with reform of direct taxation (to take effect on January 1, 2003). Legislation for the second phase of this reform will be submitted to parliament by end-October 2002 (structural benchmark). Our direct tax priorities will be to: (i) harmonize taxes on investment income; (ii) rationalize ad hoc inflation adjustments in the tax system; (iii) rationalize the system of investment incentives; and (iv) reform the system of credits against income tax. The plan will also address tax administration reform (including technical assistance needs). To achieve greater efficiency, we will reorganize the tax administration in line with the study that we have carried out with the World Bank. Conditionality on implementation will be set at the time of the first program review.

- To reform the civil service, the Council of Ministers will adopt a civil service reform strategy by end-2002. As part of the preparatory work, by end-March 2002 we will establish a ministerial committee to carry out a functional review of government, which will be completed by end-September 2002. By this time, we will also have in place an integrated system to monitor total general government and SEE employment levels on a quarterly basis (structural benchmark).

• We expect the biggest improvements in public resource use and the underlying fiscal position to arise from reductions in overstaffing, especially in inefficient SEEs. This will reduce the necessity for aggressive public sector price increases, thereby supporting disinflation, improve the efficiency of enterprises, and in many cases help to prepare the ground for privatization. Supported by a Prime Minister's circular issued on December 3, 2001, we have already initiated a voluntary retirement scheme for public sector workers. 15,000 individuals will have been retired or notified of their retirement by mid-January 2002 (prior action). We have also recently identified (with World Bank assistance) redundant workers in Türk Telekom and in the Privatization Agency portfolio of companies, and we will extend voluntary retirement offers to the individuals occupying them. For those who accept, we will provide payments, and allow them to retire, no later than end-March 2002. Also by end-January 2002, we will (i) identify all redundant workers and positions in SEEs (updating and expanding our earlier analysis); and (ii) eliminate all open, unfilled redundant positions. Through voluntary retirement offers, and layoffs only when necessary, we will reduce the number of redundant workers by one-third by end-June, and cumulatively two-thirds by end-October 2002. By end-June 2003, we will phase out the remaining redundancies. For this well-targeted attrition, we will allow no replacement hiring, and the resulting unfilled positions will be immediately eliminated. We will audit SEE compliance with this program on a quarterly basis. Progress toward meeting the above targets will also be a focus of earlier program reviews. Since we are making long-term financial savings from this action, the net cost of this initiative (severance payments less wage savings) will not be counted toward our primary surplus target, up to a limit of TL 1.25 quadrillion in 2002.

- We will enhance aggregate fiscal control, by strengthening the legal framework for fiscal policy, consolidating fiscal institutions, and deepening fiscal transparency reforms:

    - To strengthen the legal framework for fiscal policy, we will (i) pass the Law on Public Debt Management and issue two supporting communiqués, and (ii) by end-June 2002, submit to parliament a Law on Financial Management and Internal Control consistent with best international practices (structural benchmark). The latter law will cover budgeting, accounting, transparency, and internal and external control.

-   To continue the process of consolidating fiscal institutions, we will by end-March 2002, close 548 additional revolving funds (out of 1,981 remaining), to achieve the target we originally set for end-2001 (structural benchmark). We will also, in the draft budget for 2003 to be submitted to parliament, incorporate the revenue and expenditures under Law 3418. The earmarking of these revenues, and those under Law 4306 would also be eliminated. We will also improve the transparency of the operations of the remaining extra-budgetary funds (the Social Aid and Solidarity Fund, the Defense Industry Support Fund, the Privatization Fund, and the Promotion Fund). By July 2002, we will amend their governing legislation to require passage of their budgets by parliament, external audit of their accounts (reported to parliament), and monthly reporting of their accounts, on a consolidated basis, with the central government's accounts (structural benchmark). Looking forward, we will eliminate the one remaining budgetary fund (the Support Price and Stabilization Fund) in three years, when the World Bank's Agricultural Reform Implementation Project ends.

-   To enhance fiscal transparency, in the draft 2003 budget to be submitted to parliament we will (i) include net lending as an appropriation, and (ii) extend accounting and coding reforms to all consolidated budget agencies, and to general government units on a pilot basis (structural benchmark). Moreover, by end-March 2002, we will complete a survey of end-

2001 commitments in excess of appropriations (structural benchmark).

- We will enhance and better target our social spending. Already in 2002, we are increasing social spending substantially in real terms. In addition, we will address the impact of public sector retrenchment through the labor redeployment and reinsertion program (supported under the World Bank's Privatization Social Support Project), and through unemployment insurance, for which benefit payments are set to commence in 2002 (this would protect those workers who are not eligible for adequate severance). Other key priorities will be (i) to increase resources allocated to direct income support for farmers (in support of this, we will eliminate all agricultural premia in the 2003 budget), and (ii) to fully implement the World Bank supported Social Risk Mitigation Project, which seeks to enhance safety net resources available to the poorest households.

G ENHANCING THE ROLE OF THE PRIVATE SECTOR

- Our program places a special emphasis on fostering private sector development. The key elements – which have been developed in close consultation with the World Bank – include privatizing companies, encouraging domestic and foreign investment, and improving governance and transparency. We will also improve our communications policy, to underline both to the public and to investors that a genuine economic transformation is underway.

- Our privatization strategy aims to complete in 2002 the preparatory work for the divestiture of all major companies slated for sale. Besides selling enterprises for which the technical preparations have already been completed – notably TÜPRAŞ (petroleum refinery) and POAŞ (petroleum distribution) – we are committed to completing in 2002 all preparatory work for the privatization of Türk Telekom, TEKEL (tobacco and spirits), ŞEKER (sugar), THY (airlines), ERDEMIR (steel), EUAŞ (electricity generation), TEDAŞ (electricity distribution), BOTAŞ (natural gas), and state-owned land. Specifically:

- While the specific timing will depend on market conditions, we expect the Privatization Administration (PA) to proceed with the public offerings of POAŞ by end-March 2002 and the public offering of TÜPRAŞ by end-June 2002. This will lower the government's stake in TÜPRAŞ to less than 50 percent. The PA is also ready to launch the initial public offering for THY as soon as market conditions allow.

- The government has in December 2001 appointed a Privatization Tender Committee for Türk Telekom. While it was not possible for the Committee to prepare a revised privatization plan by end-2001, as originally intended, we will ensure that such a plan is adopted by the Council of Ministers in April 2002. The corporatization plan now under preparation with the help of international consultants will provide input to the privatization plan.

- On January 3, 2002, parliament passed the Tobacco Law. As the next step, a privatization plan for TEKEL will be prepared and adopted by the Council of Ministers by end-September.

- We also will proceed with the privatization of ŞEKER, with the first step being the adoption of a privatization plan by May 2002. For both TEKEL and ŞEKER, we recognize that successful privatization needs to be preceded by major operational restructuring, which we are determined to undertake in close cooperation with the World Bank.

- In the electricity sector, in January 2002,

subject to legal clarification, we expect the Council of Ministers to adopt a government decree annulling with immediate effect all the projects for which transfer of operating rights (TOOR) contracts are pending. By March 2002, the Ministry of Energy will inform the PA which electricity assets will be privatized, and by April 2002 the prequalification tenders for the distribution companies will be launched.

- We expect to complete the transfer of gas distribution companies to the PA by March 2002.

- The PA is ready to go forward with the divesting of ETI Krom AŞ, ETI Elektrometalurji AŞ, ETI Gümüs AŞ, which are in the PA portfolio, as soon as licenses are transferred from ETI Holdings.

- The PA will continue its divestment of ERDEMIR, and of tourism and fertilizer assets in its portfolio. The PA will also continue divesting its portfolio of small and medium-size companies.

- Finally, we will build on efforts made in 2001 (including legal amendments and simplified procedures) to increase the sale of government land. As constitutional problems made the legal amendments less effective than envisaged, we have initiated a study to evaluate how the remaining obstacles to government land sales could best be removed.

• We aim to make Turkey substantially more attractive for domestic and foreign investors.

• We attach the highest importance to improving governance and transparency. To this end, the Council of Ministers will adopt a strategy for increasing transparency and combating rent-seeking activities by end-January 2002 (structural benchmark).

3.4 Did the program of 2002 targeted to be implemented for three years prove successful?

Various answers can be given to the question about the success of the IMF-supported program – which began to be implemented in February 2002 – depending on different perspectives. Those who believe in the miracles of expectation management may suggest that the implementation was successful, considering the enduring vulnerability and public debt rollover in the fiscal sector. They may further claim that the decline in foreign exchange, inflation, and interest rates evidenced this success, instead of defining necessary and adequate conditions for a permanent solution. They cannot come with a solution, and tend to disguise negative developments and trends because they cannot take the risk of the cost arising from the failure of expectation management. There are two possibilities in such a case: either you attempt to strengthen through expectation management the necessary and adequate conditions technically available; or you save the day through expectation management despite the technical inadequacy and aggravating problems. While evaluating this IMF-supported program and its consequences, it proves crucial to determine which one of these two possibilites were valid at the time.

In order to determine the technical adequacy of the program and the level of success in implementation, necessary and adequate conditions should be explored first; then, it becomes obligatory to determine whether the problem, if any, arises from the program itself or from its implementation.

For a permanent solution, the system of payments should be strengthened on the one hand, and a macroeconomic balance should be established to attain the targets on the other. For this reason, structural reforms which will decrease the uncertainty by creating a sense of wholeness in the system and lead to a high rate of growth with low inflation prove crucial. Moreover, all these implementations with regard to inflation, growth, and structural reforms should be realized simultaneously. Thus, a social consensus, a strong political will, and a high-level coordination become indispensable for success.

Implementations of the IMF-supported economic program which began in February 2002 unfortunately strengthen the conviction that necessary and adequate conditions are nonexistent. While vulnerability in the system of payments does not decrease or increase, there is a rise in macroeconomic imbalance. Thus, it is attempted to disguise a probable instability in the foreign exchange, inflation, and interest rates through expectation management. With an image of artificial price stability, an indirect message that everything is going fine is conveyed. However, there is a tendency to underestimate the fact that this artificial image alone cannot play a role in decreasing the macro imbalance and the vulnerability in the system of payments as far as structural reforms are neglected. No one has ever discussed the fact that such an approach can only aggravate the problems, or this discussion is prevented. Beside international institutions such as the IMF and World Bank, the global fiscal system underestimates the situation finding various pretexts, and just recommends to carry on with the program and to pay attention to risks.

In the second quarter of 2001 when legal amendments related to structural reforms were on the agenda, an uproar broke out, and all the involved parties quarreled. However, today things seem to be different. As the deficits of the social security system widens, the burden on the budget carries on increasing. There is an attempt to meet daily needs with arbitrary and illegal implementations, and tax amnesties instead of a comprehensive tax reform. The agricultural reform aiming at increasing agricultural productivity is entirely neglected; necessary steps toward a new structure supporting the producer cannot be taken. Privatization targets cannot be attained; as the target for incomes has a priority, things do not move. Fiscal sector reform cannot be carried out properly because the policy for a gradual solution over a period of time has been adopted by necessity; vulnerability is still high. The public procurement law which would discipline the public management has been already amended twice, yet involved parties keep their silence. The problems with the public sector cannot be solved. Thus, a healthy, working system cannot be established; arbitrary applications give rise to further uncertainties. Consequently, the scarce sources cannot be efficiently used and distributed, and foreign direct investment moves in the opposite direction.

A sustainable growth becomes no more than a dream under such conditions. While the consolidated public sector primary surplus target which has been defined as a principal criterion cannot be attained, the current account deficit and savings deficit continue to widen; unrecorded economy carries on expanding. The public sector debt burden can only be alleviated by controlling the foreign exchange rate; however, the destruction caused by subsequent side effects is greater than the advantage in the medium term. Thus, the growth figures announced are far from reality.

The appreciation of the Turkish Lira which encourages the inflation and interest rates to decline in the short term leads to a decrease in interest expenditures, and prevents the public sector debt burden becoming heavier. However, it produces a negative effect on the budget revenues, unemployment, current account balance, direct investments, and growth, restricting the level of success in structural reform implementations — regardless of to what extent the government is determined to implement the reforms. Therefore, positive developments attained in certain matters cannot sustain themselves, due to the fact that problems aggravate others.

At this stage we should ask ourselves whether the situation would be different if the external loan was supplied by another source. The answer is no; similar trends would occur. In the light of this, the IMF and World Bank provide only loan support, and contribute to the expectation management, and do nothing more. Furthermore, if we are to test the current situation with different scenarios, it is not difficult to discover the truth. For instance, probable effects may be analyzed if the foreign exchange rate is increased. If the situation does not prove to be sustainable, is it possible to talk about success then?

Under these conditions, is it reasonable to suggest that the program has been adequate, and it has been successfully implemented?

It should be pointed out that Turkey's increasing importance in the international conjuncture following the September 11 attacks has its reflections on the economy. With the support of the USA, the IMF carried on backing up gradually more and more the Transition to a Stronger Economy Program after the September 11 attacks. And Turkey took second place in terms of the size of her debts. USA-backed loan support would bring relief to the Turkish economy. However, it would mean at the same time a heavy debt burden for Turkey. As a result, we have the following table. Due to her increasing debt stock Turkey became the country who received the IMF's loans with the highest interest rate, and who made the greatest contribution to the IMF's revenues.

Table 12. Loans Supplied by the IMF as of January 31, 2004
(in US $ billion)

Argentina	15.8
Brazil	28.2
Other	38.3
TURKEY	23.8

SOURCE: IMF

In this case, situations and conditions which would ensure the success of a new stabilization program should be discussed.

CHAPTER IV

Will the current program and the new program of 2005 with the IMF prove successful? How and under which conditions?

Negotiations with the IMF on the continuation of the current stabilization program and/or the shift to a newer program beginning in 2005 are still continuing in June 2004. The crucial issue in the discussions is surely the "delaying" of the repayment of Turkey's US $19.5 billion debt which is due in 2005 and 2006. These developments must be analyzed from different perspectives, but first, we should look on page 6 of the informative notice by the Central Bank of Turkey under the title "The Basic Characteristics of the Inflationary Process, The Inflation in January and Future Expectations": "Starting from mid-October 2001, the prospects of achieving fiscal discipline in 2002, the persistence in structural reforms and the impending additional external financing from the IMF have eliminated the concerns about the sustainability of domestic debts and have changed economic expectations into positive. As a result of the change in expectations, interest rates declined substantially and the bubble in the exchange rate, emerged during the summer 2001, has burst".

Leaving "the prospects of achieving fiscal discipline in 2002 and the persistence in structural reforms" part aside as a reason to stir up hopes, we can continue with our evaluation: Additional financing support by the IMF has had a positive effect on the interest rates and domestic debt rollover. However, we must not forget the historical fact that, particularly starting from 1990, the decline in the interest rates and subsequent relief in its pressure on the domestic debts have always been linked to foreign financing opportunities. In other words, whenever Turkey felt comfortable with foreign finances, a decline in the interest rates was observed. We should admit this fact primarily.

Any agreement with the IMF that will be implemented from February 2005, will be a continuation of the program which has been implemented since the beginning of 2002, because the discussions are mainly focused on the primary surplus – whether it should be 6.5 percent and/or less than this – and the delaying of the debt repayments. These discussions point out that the "well-known" program will be implemented as it is.

At this point, in order to elaborate the possibilities of success of the current and the new program which will be continued in 2005, we have to determine certain basic assumptions which are the prerequisites of a program basically relying on foreign financing support, and analyze and discuss the conditions for their success. These assumptions can be listed as follows:

- Turkey should avoid any kind of "stress" that would involve political risks, and achieve a wide range consensus throughout society.

- Economic relations with the neighboring countries should be improved, expanding joint interests. The position and the function of Turkey in GMEP (Greater Middle East Project) should not create any risk.

- The structural problems in the world must change in a way that would not stir up any crisis in Turkey. Any kind of economic or political crisis that would create uncertainty should not take place, a fair competitive environment should be attained and sustainable growth should continue.

- For a sustainable growth, structural reforms must be implemented.

- Every year a sizeable (US \$7–8 billion) amount of Foreign Direct Investment must be attracted to the country. And the incoming capital must not only meet domestic demand, but also contribute to exports and employment.

- Turkish Lira must not be overvalued.

- Long-term domestic and foreign debts must be found, and costs must be decreased.

- There must be a net positive primary surplus in a stable growing economy without restricting social needs.

Now let us elaborate the assumptions listed above and discuss their chances of success.

4.1 Turkey should avoid any kind of "stress" that would involve political risks and achieve a wide range consensus throughout society

We must not forget that the success of the current and/or a similar program with the IMF is closely linked to the avoidance of the stress that would invoke political risks. The most important condition for the economic program's success is to prevent any kind of risks which may cause clashes between different sectors. The political risk should be perceived not only as a risk between "high-level" political parties, but also as any lack of consensus between different interest groups.

One of the major problems of Turkey is the growing lack of communication among the real, fiscal and public sectors. This increases the uncertainty for future expectations. The high indebtedness rate in the public sector and the lack of equity of the fiscal sector reduce sensitivity towards the problems of the real sector; the labor-intensive sectors being the first of all, the real sector can hardly breathe. The exchange rate continues to be in the heart of conflicting interests.

The increase in the exchange rate, that is, the depreciation of the Turkish Lira cannot be tolerated by either the public or the fiscal sector. Consequently, the burden of the public debt increases. If the situation sustains, the domestic and foreign debt instruments of the Treasury will lose their value, leading to a situation where the debts cannot be managed. Nobody even wants to think about the effect of this possibility on the balance of payments of the fiscal sector. The current expectation management is shaped according to these compulsory needs; while straining the market trends suitable for the positions of the public and the fiscal sectors, the macroeconomic inequilibrium is not taken into consideration out of necessity. The externally supported fiscal and public sectors are striving to write over-optimistic scenarios. To sum up, the Turkish Lira should continue to appreciate and the inflation and interest rates to decrease.

Nobody can say anything against the decrease of the inflation and the interest rates but we cannot accept the dragging of the real sector into the crisis with full throttle either. As long as the domestic demand declines and the competitive power of the domestic products decreases, the problems will continue to accumulate. The problem of replacing the companies, particularly in the labor-intensive sectors, which cannot continue to operate, arises. As the Turkish Lira appreciates, unrecorded economy and the smuggling of goods through the borders remain the questions to be answered. While unemployment increases and the factor revenues decrease, the control over the increasing public sector deficits continues to be a major problem. These questions and similar ones are not taken seriously by the public and fiscal sectors or by the IMF and other international institutions.

The Turkish Lira continues to appreciate; as the dollar appreciates in the international markets and remains constant in the domestic market, the real sector continues to struggle. The demolishing effects on the real sector of increasing raw material prices in the international markets, the overvalued Turkish Lira, and the increasing domestic input costs will create social and political problems for which nobody knows the solutions.

We know that everything that could be done, has already been tried by the real sector; both the labor and capital productivity have been increased. Great risks have been taken in order to survive; the capacities have been forced to the limit to reduce the costs even at the sacrifice of profits. Despite all these attempts, if they cannot continue, then there is not much left to be done. If their voice is not heard as strong as it used to be, this does not mean that they are in good condition, but in fact, that they have become much weaker than they used to be. As they run out of hope, they need to think from a different perspective. The decreasing inflation and interest rates cannot solve their problems. It is widely accepted that the crisis in the real sector is preferred to the fiscal sector crisis in order to gain some time. They do not trust the ones who have chosen this option. The real sector is neither interested in taking the date for the EU membership talks, nor in the new arrangement with the IMF for the period after 2004. Before the eighth review the IMF delegation can say that for the first time they see the real sector "complaining so much". It seems that while the public and the fiscal sectors travel in the same boat the others are in another because the clash of interests between the real sector and the others cannot be prevented.

The crucial element of a stabilization program is the social consensus. The reflection of conflicting interests between the parties such as employee-employer, real sector-fiscal sector, agricultural sector-industrial sector, public-private sectors, cannot be positive on the economy. For instance, to put the burden of the economic program on a specific party's shoulders may easily endanger the social consensus. If all the involved parties do not "sacrifice" all together, sooner or later the social consensus will be ruined.

A lack of social consensus will bring social uneasiness, an environment where the social balance has been destroyed. The conflict of interests intensifies. The stronger ones try to utilize the economic environment for their own sake of gains, as long as they get the opportunity. Whereas the social consensus minimizes this kind of clash within the society. By means of social consensus, it is possible to register the unrecorded economy and spread the sacrifice to all levels of the society. The struggle between the employee and the employer can only be eased in this way. Society's willingness to pay tax can also be evaluated from this perspective. In brief, we must not forget that the social consensus is the foundation of permanent stability and increased productivity.

4.2 Economic relations with the neighboring countries should be improved, expanding joint interests. The position and function of Turkey in GMEP (Greater Middle East Project) should not create any risk

The foundations of the "global restructuring" process which has begun in the twenty-first century, started to be laid in 1989 when the Berlin Wall collapsed. The order of the bipolar world was changing. The 1997 Asian Crisis and the terrorist attack on September 11, 2001, significantly helped the USA become the hegemonic power of the unipolar world.

The decrease in the Asia-Pacific demand with the Asian Crisis and the loss of power in the Japanese economy caused contraction in the world trade and capital movements. While the global demand was shrinking, the USA remained the most important center for the demand and thus strengthened its power over the other nations. Certainly, the USA being the most important demand center was not a very healthy development for its economy. As it will be discussed later, the USA economy would face great amounts of deficits and its indebtedness would increase dramatically in that process. And the sustainability of these deficits and debts would occupy the agenda.

The attacks of September 11 have also changed the security strategies of the USA Terror and mass destruction weapons constituted the targets of the new national security strategy. Within the scope of this, a new global restructuring for the next twenty years, would be discussed. The region beginning from Gibraltar, including North Africa, reaching up to the Pacific Ocean on the East, would accommodate almost two thirds of the world population and the major energy resources in the next twenty or thirty years. The new initiative of the USA administration of "gradual reforming" was called the "Greater Middle East Project". The first step of the project was conducting reforms in politics, security areas, energy issues and economics in the generic sense, in the countries of the region.

Middle East Partnership Initiative (MEPI) was the political tool of this new forward strategy. MEPI champions more democratic governments and separation of religion from governance; supports education and information systems that enable all people, including girls, to acquire the knowledge and skills necessary to compete in today's economy and improve the quality of their lives; and works toward economic, political, and educational systems where women enjoy full and equal opportunities. On the other hand, Global Defense Posture (GDP) involves the maximum security of the region which extends from Poland to Afghanistan. The security of the energy resources is the most important pillar of this realignment process. Millennium Challenge Account (MCA) funds initiatives to improve the economies and standards of living in qualified developing countries. The goal of the MCA is to reward sound policy decisions that support economic growth and reduce poverty. In order to establish trade integration in the region, Middle East Trade Initiative (MEFTI) and Middle East Trade Area (MEFTA) have been proposed by the USA; new initiatives are taken to expand the free trade agreements between Morocco and Bahrain to include 21 countries and their integration with the World Trade Organization. By means of the National Energy Strategy the USA aims at reducing its dependence upon the oil of this region until 2020. Securing the energy resources and the routes, realizing the East-West Energy corridor are some components of the strategy.

GMEP in particular was the most important item on the agenda of the NATO summit which took place in Turkey at the end of June 2004. The USA expressed its desire to have general support for the project during the summit, and thus, the project went into effect.

It is obvious that Turkey has important roles in this so-called restructuring process. Turkey, which is sometimes referred to as a model for the region countries, is one of the most important balancing elements in the relations between the region countries and the US. In this manner, if Turkey stands against the GMEP, it is highly plausible that the global equilibrium will be ruined.

On the other hand, if she agrees to be a part of the project, she will lead to a political alliance with the USA.

For Turkey, to resist GMEP naturally constitutes a serious risk. However, to be a part of it may also constitute an equally serious risk because during the application of this project, the USA with the aim to create conditions for democracy, may support certain groups and/or provoke them to revolt against their rulers in a secret or open manner, and may subsequently trigger chaos and terror in the region, which still has a kind of feudal system based on landlords. *The probability of the failure of the USA to create democracy out of chaos constitutes one of the most important risks for Turkey.* In brief, if the project fails when Turkey is part of it, Turkey will be in trouble in the region. Whatever the percentage of the probability is, this should be perceived as a serious risk.

Without any doubt, another risk is whether the USA will maintain her "hegemonic power" in the next twenty-fifty year period. The following table points to the possibility of shifts in the global balance in the future.

Table 13. Power Resources in the World

	USA	Japan	Germany	France	Britain	Russia	China	India
Territory in thousands km^2	9,269	378	357	547	245	17,075	9,597	3,288
Population in millions	276	127	83	59	60	146	1,262	1,014
Nuclear warheads (1999)	12,070	0	0	450	192	22,500	>40	85–90
Military Budget in billions of dollars (1999)	288.8	41.1	24.7	29.5	34.6	31	12.6	10.7
Military Personnel	1,371,500	236,300	332,800	317,300	212,400	1,004,100	2,480,000	1,173,000
GDP in billions of dollars in purchasing power parity (1999)	9,255	2,950	1,864	1,373	1,290	620	4,800	1,805
Per capita GDP (PPP, 1999)	33,900	23,400	22,700	23,300	21,800	4,200	3,800	1,800
High-tech exports in billions of dollars (1997)	637	420	112	69	96	87	183	32

SOURCE: JOSEPH S. NYE. 2002 *THE PARADOX OF AMERICAN POWER.* OXFORD: OXFORD UNIVERSITY PRESS, P. 37.

In his work *The Paradox of American Power*, Joseph S. Nye explains that the United States can remain the leading power in world politics in the twenty-first century and beyond. However, this depends upon some assumptions such as: "It assumes that the long-term productivity of the American economy will be sustained, that American society will not decay, that the United States will maintain its military strength but not become over militarized, that Americans will not become so unilateral and arrogant in their strength that they squander the nation's considerable fund of soft power, that there will not be some catastrophic series of events that profoundly transforms American attitudes in an isolationist direction, and that Americans will define their national interest in a broad and farsighted way that incorporates global interests…" (170, 171).

However, there are others who are not so optimistic about the future of the United States. One of them is a Professor of Economics at Colombia University, Jeffrey D. Sachs. In his article entitled "The Decline of America", he explains the situation in which currently the USA is, and the possible risks involved:

But despite its wealth and military might, America's ability to project political power – for good or ill – will decline in future years, for at least five reasons:

- *America's budget is in crisis.* Thanks to Bush's tax cuts and military spending, which have contributed to budget deficits of $500 billion per year, the US will have to raise taxes and limit budget spending, whether or not Bush is re-elected. The annual military budget, which has increased by $150 billion since Bush took office, will need to be cut in coming years to get the budget under control;

- *The US is borrowing massively from abroad.* Asia's central banks have bought hundreds of billions of dollars of US securities. Japan alone has foreign exchange reserves of around $750 billion, much of that in US treasury bills. China, Hong Kong, India, Korea, Singapore, and Taiwan together have another $1.1 trillion or so in reported foreign exchange reserves. In short, the US is in deep and growing debt to Asia. Only massive buying of treasury bills by Asian central banks has prevented the dollar from falling even more precipitously than it has;

- *The rest of the world is catching up.* America's big technological lead will narrow relative to Brazil, China, India, and other major economic regions of the developing world. China will have an economy larger than the US economy within 25 years – potentially 50% larger by 2050. India, considerably poorer on average than China, will also close the wealth gap. By 2050, India will conceivably have an economy the size of America's, with four times the population and roughly one-fourth of the average income level per person;

- *A narrower economic gap will reduce America's relative geopolitical power.* China and India, which together account for about 40% of the world's population, will begin to play much larger roles on the world scene. The current xenophobic reactions to "outsourcing" of jobs to India's software engineers – a hot political issue in the US – reflects the underlying anxiety of a US population that wants to stay in the economic lead. With or without American protectionism, Asia's technological capacities and incomes will grow. This will be good for the world because prosperity will be more widely spread, even if America's ego gets hurt in the process.

- *Demographics will weaken America's militaristic approach to the world.* Much of Bush's support comes from white fundamentalist Christian men. This, in my opinion, is a social group that is fighting a rearguard battle against the growing social power of women, immigrants, and other religions. It is also fighting against secularism, such as the teaching of modern biology and evolutionary theory. The religious right's backward-looking agenda – and the Manichaean worldview that underlies it – is doomed. The US Census Bureau recently found that by 2050, the non-Hispanic white population of the US is likely to be only half of the total US population, down from 69% currently. By 2050, 24% of the population will be Hispanic, 14% will be African-American, and 8% Asian. The US will look more like the world, especially Latin America.

- In the face of these five factors, the dream of global empire held by many US right-wingers will most likely fade. This may happen sooner rather than later if Bush loses this November in an election that is certain to be very close. But whatever the outcome, the US cannot postpone forever its inevitable decline relative to the rest of the world.

Sachs is quite pessimistic about the future of the GMEP of the USA, which is one of the most crucial factors that will affect the uncertainty in the region, and he refutes Nye's assumptions for the United States to maintain its hegemonic power. Without a doubt, this is a sign of a serious uncertainty for the region, and subsequently for Turkey. In addition, we must mention that the United States' "so-called" initiative of giving the government to the Iraqis, is not perceived to be convincing by the Middle Eastern people.

4.3 Structural Problems

The structural problems in the world must change in a way that would not stir up any crisis in Turkey. Any kind of economic or political crisis that would create uncertainty should not take place, a fair competitive environment should be attained and sustainable growth should continue.

As the world economy globalizes, the problems and/or crises – regardless of their intensity – which the countries encounter, have influences on other countries. The structural problems such as, hunger, epidemics like AIDS, countries becoming more dependent as a result of droughts and soils turned into deserts by the global heating, the imbalance in the incomes of the northern and the southern hemispheres, millions of people trying to survive on only one dollar per day, unfair income distribution, insufficient demand to meet the increase in production provided by the developments in technology, regional wars and their devastating effects, agricultural output that cannot keep pace with the population increase, collapsing social security systems, and so on, continue to jeopardize the world economy. However, steps toward the solutions of these problems cannot be taken because of the power balances. The countries dedicate, if they can, only a small portion of their large military budgets to the solutions of these structural problems.

On the other hand, the world economy has been experiencing

a new monetary system in the framework of a free exchange rate. The former system which was established in 1944 was free of the exchange rate and interest risks. But today these risks come along with serious uncertainties in the world in which capital movements have been liberalized. The economies of the countries are compelled to sustain a stable, continuous growth in an environment of uncertainties. The globalization trend is pushing the countries or sectors which "are not ready" to face the fierce competition. The frequently emerging crises are jeopardizing the fluidity of the capital movements. Under these circumstances, countries such as Turkey, which are dependent upon foreign finance and/or cannot sustain macroeconomic equilibriums without the foreign financing support, are put under pressure.

Without any doubt, the world conjuncture is of vital importance for the success of the current economic program. It is crucial for the public sector, which has pre-scheduled sizeable debt repayments, primarily to the IMF, in 2005 and 2006, to find funds at reasonable costs in international markets. Now, how can a development that may have influence on the international finance markets in the forthcoming period, affect Turkey? We should elaborate this in relation with the world conjuncture:

a. Primarily let us point to the international developments: The United States Economy Administration has pulled down the short-term interest rates to the 1 percent level for the first time in 50 years, and applied massive tax cuts, in order to come out of the recession of 2001. The decline in the short-term interest rates down to 1 percent, led the institutions to take short-term loans and then purchase long-term bonds and/or securities because the institutions were racing to get the most benefit from the differences in the short- and long-term interest rates. The general decline in the interest rates did not only revive the securities market, but also the real estate market. Massive tax cuts combined with robust budget deficits and decline in the interest rates revitalized the economy, and consequently inflationist trends started to emerge. Inflation data of the USA point up to 3 percent.

b. US $500 billion of budget deficit and the equal amount of trade deficit of the USA are called "twin deficits" and is a world record. Under these circumstances, FED has given signs of a probable raise in the interest rates. The increase in the interest rates seems inevitable now: new increases will probably follow the 0.25 percent increments in June and August 2004. The question here is the size of steps and the rates of the increases. Will the interest rates remain around 3.5 percent within the next two years or will they rise up to around 6.5 percent again? On the other hand, will the increase in the USA's interest rates trigger the same for other countries?

c. It is difficult to reply to the question regarding the increase in the interest rates, while on the other hand we can provide some explanations for the other questions in the light of the reflections in the markets. Announcing an informative notice about the interest rates such as "the increase is possible," FED has warned the institutional investors to be careful. The financial markets have responded to this move, and as a result, 10–year treasury bonds of the USA have entered an increased trend. Similar reflections have appeared in the Eurobonds of the developing countries. Beginning with Brazil, all bonds of the countries have been sold, naturally including those of Turkey: without any change in the credibility note of Turkey, the incomes of the Eurobond have reached 10 percent level from 8 percent. Of course, the developments have not been restricted to the Eurobonds. The interest rates of the Government Domestic Debt Instruments (GDDI) have also increased, resulting in voluminous sales and increase in the exchange rates over 15 percent, in other words, the TL has depreciated. Thus the primary reflection of the increase signal in the US interest rates has been on the borrowing costs. From now on, the level of these costs will be dependent upon the FED's decisions for the level of the interest rates. Within this framework, we encounter another question: will the results of the increase in the interest rates in the USA be limited to the increase in the borrowing costs or will they involve other problems in finding foreign financing?

d. Another problem which is affecting the world economy is the price of oil, which currently fluctuates within US $35–40 band. The oil prices are highly susceptible to the increases of the world oil demand, primarily to the increase of the consumption in China. On the other hand, being the target of global terrorism, the oil pipelines and the employees of this industry constitute another pressure on the prices. The markets are familiar with the US $35–40 band. The increase of the oil prices does not only increase the costs, but also causes a flow of the funds from oil dependent countries such as Turkey to the oil exporting countries. We know that the cost of oil for Turkey has increased by around US $1.4 billion.

e. Both the increase of the oil prices and the expectations of the interest rates have similar medium-term economic results: the spoiled global income distribution, the shrinking international trade volume, increase in unemployment, widening of the budget deficits, and volatility of the cash flows in jeopardizing levels, deterioration in the institution structure as a result of the devaluation of the securities and the real estates can be the primary negative consequences. Under the current circumstances, it seems not possible to compensate these negative effects of either the oil prices or the interest rates by adjusting one or the other. In other words, to claim that it is not necessary to raise the interest rates because of the recession which will be caused by the high oil prices, will not be a realistic approach, for the current inflationary pressure is not based on demand, but on cost. We must point to the fact that, as the oil prices increase, the increase in the medium-term interest rates will also be higher.

f. The dramatic increase in the raw material prices, due to the growth rate – first of all in China with a level of 9 percent – and the developments in demand, constitute another problem for the world economy. For the time being, Turkey does not feel this price pressure which is jeopardizing the cost structures of the countries, because of the over-valued TL. However, this must be anticipated as a threat.

THE CURRENT SITUATION AND DEVELOPMENTS IN THE WORLD ECONOMY

THE ECONOMIC SITUATION AND TRENDS IN THE USA

- The transition from recession to growth and its sustainability is the most important problem that the USA economy is dealing with.

- For two years, the US $200 billion war expenditures may be good for growth, but the current situation of the dollar and widening budget deficits (up to 5 percent of GNP) are perceived as signals of a forthcoming crisis. On the other hand, the foreign trade deficit as much as the budget deficit that is, the twin deficits are driving the USA economy. The USA economy deficit is financed by other countries including primarily Japan and China. For instance, China had purchased an amount of US $100 billion of USA Treasury debt instruments.

- Widening budget deficits, increasing defense expenditures and the cost of the overseas operations, increase in the non-operational incomes of the institutions, the activity in the construction sector thanks to the lowered costs, overturning to a negative trend in savings, cost pressure because of the increase in the goods' prices, instability and volatility in the exchange rates are deepening the structural problems of the US economy...

- We will see how prepared the markets are for the FED's intention of increasing the interest rates and the possible risks aftermath, in the following periods as Greenspan has already given the signal and warned the markets. Without a doubt the outcome of this development will produce negative effects first of all on the USA and on the developing countries such as Turkey and then on all the countries of the world, because if the interest rates increase, the market prices of all the securities (bonds, Eurobonds, stocks, and so on) will reduce. This trend will affect the real estate sector, too. For this reason, there is a strong perception of the global avoidance of such investments...

ECONOMIC SITUATION AND TRENDS
IN THE EU REGION

- The recession that has been continuing since the beginning of 1990, unemployment and the population growing old, are among the main problems of the EU.

- The decline in domestic demand in the German economy which started particularly in mid-2000 and is still continuing along with the global recession, affects the EU indexes negatively, because Germany is known as the locomotive of the EU. Before overcoming the difficulties of joining, the increasing oil and raw materials prices has put Germany in a difficult position since the beginning of 2000. The unemployment rate in Germany was 9.3 percent in 2003 whereas it was 9.5 percent in France.

- With the implementation of the Euro in twelve EU member countries in 2002, the prices of basic food and other consumer goods have increased by around 30 percent. Similar developments have been observed in the service sector, too. This of course meant the weakening of the purchasing power of the Europeans.

- The continuous decline in industrial production, especially due to the increasing costs and incapability to create substitute areas deepened the recession and unemployment.

- Chronic budget deficits even caused the questioning of the economic EU criteria. Germany and France, each with over 4 percent deficit, have already exceeded the limits which were set by the criteria. And the entrance of the new countries into the Union will worsen the situation.

- The problem of increasing the interest rates in the EU, in parallel with the USA, will cause the Euro to depreciate with a subsequent reflection of the cost factor on the European market.

- Consequently, the stagflation trend, and foreign and domestic policies in parallel with the USA are affecting the trends and the future of the EU...

CURRENT SITUATION AND DEVELOPMENTS
IN THE JAPANESE ECONOMY

- Japan, experiencing recession since 1990, entered into a deep financial crisis with the 1997 Asian crisis. Failing to re-collect their credits in Asia, the Japanese banks could only stand by the state support.

- For a few years, there has been a growth trend because of the appreciated Yen, but unemployment continues to be a problem (1980 2%, 2003 6%).

- Because of the regional competition, industrial production power is still weakening. The Japanese industry was founded on the basis of serial production, but the trends in the world moved towards the variability, high technology, and service-oriented structure.

- The problems of the fiscal sector are still prevailing. While the banks are trying to overcome the problem of the re-collection of credits, the public sector on the other hand, is trying to keep them operating. As known, in order to secure the future of the Japanese economy, the state resources were being used, but with the widening budget deficits up to 8 percent of the GNP, the state has been stuck in deep debt. The ratio of the government debt to GNP has reached up to 140 percent.

- With its US $4 trillion GNP, Japan is the largest economy after the US and experiencing serious problems in activating its domestic market which constitutes 85 percent of the economy. Yielding a foreign trade surplus, Japan cannot get the consumers' confidence in the domestic market to increase demand. While the interest rates are negative in the country, saving is almost punished and investing and/or using credits are encouraged. Yet this huge economy cannot put domestic demand into motion. Thus, the global problems are immediately reflected on the Japanese economy.

CURRENT SITUATION AND TRENDS IN THE CHINESE ECONOMY

- After opening to the world markets in 1978, China has achieved a yearly average 8 percent growth rate for the last 25 years. 16 percent of the total growth of the world economy in 2002 was provided by the Chinese economy alone. Along with high-tech products, China has become a strategic country in the production of labor-oriented products.

- Exports and domestic revenues continue with an increasing trend in domestic demand.

- Inflation is around 3.3 percent, the currency has been pegged to the dollar since 1995. For this reason, the dollar's depreciation against the Euro also causes the depreciation of the Chinese currency and strengthens its competitive power. (By depreciating its currency by 30 percent in 1995, it overcame the Asian crisis. Now \$1 = 8.28 Yuan.)

- It is a favorable location for the foreign direct investments. Due to the low labor costs and other advantages, many countries are losing their manufacturing industries to China. Therefore, China has a great share in the international foreign direct investment market. The increasing trends in investments regardless of the supply, the improved investment environment are pushing the entire world to invest in China.

- China is strengthening its military and political structure in a global sense.

- With an investment effort in 1998, China is implementing a 10-year US \$1 trillion investment project and aiming to attract foreign direct investment of at least half of this amount.

- Its share in the world trade is continuously increasing and with the growth trend, China is increasing the raw materials imports. While the ratio of China's share in the world's exports was 3.9 percent in 2000, she managed to increase this share to over 6 percent. A similar trend is observed in the imports, too. For instance, South Korea and Taiwan export more to China than to the USA.

- China was relieving the inflationist pressure particularly in the USA, with its industrial exports, but with the giant leap in China's imports and economic growth, the world has now encountered a China-oriented cost pressure.

- China seems to be the most successful country in protecting herself from the dangers and utilizing the opportunities. Increasing interest rates in the world also contribute to this trend.

Lessons from America's Fiscal Recklessness

by Jeffrey D. Sachs

George W. Bush has done more to wreck US economic policy than any other President in American history, exceeding even his mentor, Ronald Reagan. In just three years in office, he has destroyed a fragile political consensus that had taken a decade to construct, and that could take another decade to re-create. In doing so, Bush has risked America's long-term economic health and social stability. Because the long-term budgetary challenges that the US is so badly mismanaging are not unique, America's fiscal blunders provide important lessons for other countries.

The main problem with fiscal policy is that politicians can easily make themselves temporarily popular by cutting taxes and increasing public spending while running up massive public debts, leaving repayment to the future. This trick can last a few years, but sooner rather than later budget deficits and growing public debt force a painful policy reversal. Yet a cynical politician can buy himself re-election and perhaps be in retirement when the crisis arrives.

One would imagine that after hundreds of such

episodes of fiscal irresponsibility around the world in recent decades, voters would be allergic to such tricks. Yet Bush is doing it again, buying popularity today by doling out massive tax cuts while simultaneously increasing military spending and even raising expenditure on education and health. The result is a budget deficit equivalent to more than 5% of GDP.

What's worse is that America's long-term budgetary prospects were already troubling before Bush began his reckless policies. The US population is aging, so there will be a sharp increase in the costs of publicly funded health care and pension systems. Careful calculations show that future revenues under the tax policies favored by Bush are likely to fall tens of trillions of dollars short of the costs of public pensions, health care, and other fiscal spending expected by the public.

At some point in the future, there will thus need to be steep increases in tax collections, sharp cuts in public spending, or both, to correct Bush's actions. So why does the public support his policies? Because the public has little understanding or concern about these long-term consequences, even though they will eventually hurt most Americans.

The richest taxpayers are, of course, happy because they received the bulk of the tax cuts. Amazingly, the richest 5% of US taxpayers received almost half of the tax cuts, and these rich taxpayers clearly expect the other 95%--the middle class and the poor--to bear most of the future spending cuts and tax increases. Meanwhile, Bush has convinced many poor and middle-class voters that they should be happy, too, without telling them that they will have to pay for their small tax cuts with much larger cuts in future government services if his administration's policies prevail in the long term.

If Americans had a political memory, they would understand that they already rode this fiscal "roller coaster" once in the past 20 years. Ronald Reagan also came to office promising massive tax cuts and large increases in military spending. The result was a huge budget deficit by the middle of the 1980's.

Tax cuts made Reagan enormously popular and helped win him re-election in 1984. It then took over a decade--starting in Reagan's second term, and continuing through the terms of George Bush, Sr. and Bill Clinton--to get the budget back to surplus. Of course, this meant approving fresh tax increases, which cost George Bush, Sr. his re-election and led to the polarized politics of the 1990's.

History will almost certainly repeat. Some right-wing ideologues in the Bush administration believe that today's budget deficits will eventually force government social spending to be cut sharply. They hope to dismantle programs such as Social Security and Medicare. But the US public strongly supports these social programs. So the right-wing strategy of cutting taxes first in order to force cuts in social programs later will fail, and eventually tax rates will have to rise.

Others in the Bush administration argue that tax cuts are important for pulling the US out of recession. This argument is also mistaken. America's economy could have recovered without the tax cuts, and perhaps even more robustly. In any event, it is a huge mistake to base long-term tax policies on the short-run business cycle.

There are two vital lessons for other countries. The first is that the looming US budget deficits will sooner or later limit America's international power. Americans supported the Iraq war only because they didn't have to pay for it with increased taxes. When Americans are forced to choose between foreign adventures and higher taxes, they will be much less likely to support expensive military operations abroad. Indeed, the US will be deeply divided internally as the public grapples with the fiscal mess left by Bush.

The second lesson is that countries ought to plan their budgets taking into account the rising fiscal costs of an aging population. Long-term budgetary conditions are rarely in clear view of taxpayers or the parliament.

Governments should be required to submit long-term budget assessments together with their annual budget proposals, in order to reduce the tendency towards short-run political manipulation of the budget.

The US can serve as an early warning to other countries. The White House ought to provide others with the same caveat that magicians on television give their viewers: "Do not try this at home."

(Sachs, December 2002)

4.4 Structural reforms must be implemented for a sustainable growth

In recent years, there has been a lot of discussion about structural reforms in Turkey; however, they have been widely resisted and not understood properly. Even though the implementation of structural reforms is a basic condition to attain a stable, internationally competitive and productive economy, it has become an abstract subject the importance of which has not been comprehended. The efforts to implement such reforms were either incomplete or alienated from the realities of this country.

Turkey was being governed by a system in which "everything was controlled by" the politics; the economy was utilized for political ends (for example, for vote maximization), the legal system was intervened in by the politicians and disregarded. However, the rule of law must have been supreme and equally applied for everyone; the economy must have been structured under fair competitive conditions and must have attained productivity while the politics must have behaved accordingly. The main aim of the structural reforms was to convert the political supremacy into a legal supremacy.

The crucial error made in the implementation of the reforms, was their partial and incomplete application and the use of the trial and error method. However, we must emphasize that the entirety of the reforms was extremely important for their effectiveness and for the transformation of the structure.

If we draw the picture:

- First of all, it is necessary to implement legal reform. A legal system which is fast and effective and suitable for the changing conditions of the world, is a pre-requisite for structural reforms.

- The sectors which are currently controlled by politics: agriculture, fiscal system, social security system, public administrations and bureaucracy, tax system, Central Bank, energy sector, State Economic Enterprises (SEE) must be restructured, and the legal system will be adapted according to this restructuring.

- Of these issues, it is not enough to concentrate for instance only on privatization and/or agriculture. An entirety must be achieved. And this entirety will also include the removal of the obstacles to these structural reforms. Primarily, the most important obstacle, the political mentality must change; while, on the other hand, the economic uncertainties must be eliminated through education of society and social consensus. All these efforts should concentrate on achieving a sustainable growth so that problems such as unemployment, public debt, insufficient savings sources and weak fiscal structure can be overcome.

Why are the structural reforms necessary?
- To achieve transparency.

- To minimize corruption.

- To establish a healthy competition environment for the effective use and distribution of the scarce resources.

However, in spite of all these main targets, in the second quarter of 2001 when the legal arrangements related to the structural reforms were the current issue, an uproar broke out, and all the involved parties quarreled, causing deep confusion in society. Today, we notice that the IMF is not as insistent as it was in 2001 on the implementation of structural reforms. Criticisms against the IMF's social policies and the changing international political strategies of the USA after the September 11 attacks have had a great influence on this. Yet, as long as the deficits of the social security system widen, the pressure on the budget increases. Instead of a comprehensive tax reform, arbitrary and illegal practices along with tax amnesties are implemented to meet the daily demands. Agricultural reform which should aim at increasing agricultural productivity is currently being neglected entirely; with ignorance and with systems which are alien to Turkey's conditions, the producers cannot get support for increasing productivity. The privatization targets are still far out of reach; since the income target has priority, things do not move. The fiscal reform cannot be carried out properly because the policy for a gradual solution over a period of time has been adopted; the vulnerability is still high. The public procurement law which was prepared to discipline the public administration, has already been amended twice and diverted from its target, yet nobody wants to talk about it. The problems with the public administration continue. As a result of all these negative developments, a healthy, working system cannot be established; with arbitrary applications the uncertainties are increased. In this case, the effective use and distribution of the scarce resources prove impossible and foreign direct investment moves in the opposite direction to where it should be directed. But, we know that sustainable stability is closely linked to the structural reforms, and that it is only possible to achieve medium-term and permanent improvement in this way.

4.5 Every year a sizeable (US $7–8 billion) amount of foreign direct investment must be attracted to the country. And the incoming capital must not only meet domestic demand but also contribute to exports and employment

We have already discussed the destructive influence of growth by means of consumer credits and domestic demand, on the current account trade balance in the previous sections. One of the primary problems of Turkey is to finance the current account deficit, whereas the other is unemployment...

The financing of the current account deficit essentially

comprises short-term borrowing and hot money under the net errors and omissions item. For instance, an amount of US $4.9 billion of the current account deficit of US $6.8 billion in 2003 was compensated by a foreign currency inflow of which the source was unknown, as it can be observed in the balance of payments statistics of the Central Bank. However, the Asian crisis showed that the sustainability over the medium- and long-term of the current account deficit funded with hot money and/or money with an unknown source was rather uncertain. Since the current account deficit is projected to reach US $10 billion in 2004, and the same vulnerable funds are possibly going to be used to close this deficit, uneasiness and uncertainty about the future increase.

The role of foreign capital in financing the current account deficit and solving the unemployment problem is certainly gaining importance because the current and the new IMF programs are based on the appreciation of the TL.

Both the current program and the three-year program to be implemented from the beginning of 2005 are based on the inflow of foreign capital. Behind the steps taken by Turkey to enter the EU in the last two years and her attempts to adapt to the global trends lays the expectation of foreign capital inflow. By the second half of 2004, we can say that the 2000 program has been unproductive in bringing in foreign capital. However, we must also note that the financing of the current account deficit and relief of the unemployment problem are closely linked to the foreign capital inflow by the very nature of this program because Turkey is not strong enough to realize these targets by means of her own dynamics, within the framework of the implemented program. On the other hand, instead of exploring such potential dynamics the program is sacrificing existing ones in order to manage the public sector debt.

4.6 Turkish lira must not be overvalued

As we have already mentioned while analyzing the three-year arrangement of 2002 with the IMF, Turkey would act according to the export-based growth model. This point is important because Turkey, having difficulty in attracting foreign capital, should at least protect her competitive power and be careful with the trade deficit. Turkey must inevitably learn from the 1997 crises which started in Asia and spread to Russia and Brazil that the current account deficit financed with hot money can only be sustainable for the short-term, however, the result in the medium- and long-terms is a financial crisis. In order for a country to increase her competitive power and to avoid substantial trade deficit, the depreciation of the national currency is not the only solution. An increase in productivity can also eliminate the negative effects of the appreciated currency on the trade deficit, and equip the country with a competitive power.

First, the appreciation of the TL and its effects should be explored, and Turkey's competitive power should be discussed in relation with this.

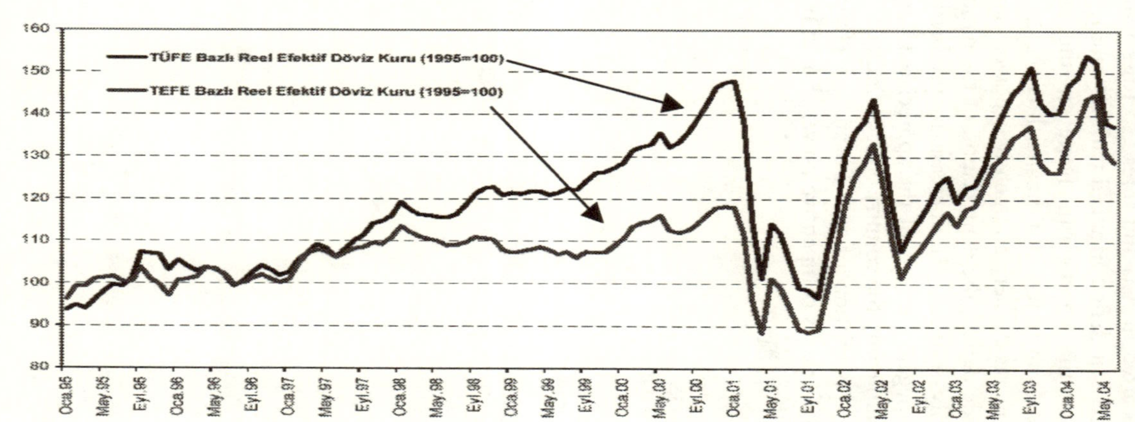

Graph 10. Real Effective Exchange Rates (Is the Turkish Lira appreciated?)

SOURCE: CRBT

a. One of the parameters which indicate the competitive power in foreign trade, is known to be the real effective exchange rate. The Central Bank of Turkey calculates the real effective exchange rate for both WPI and CPI on the basis of the year 1995. In short, by comparing Turkey's inflation must be with those of the countries with which Turkey has trade relations or competes, the assumed foreign exchange rate is calculated. According to this approach, the change in the exchange rate must be roughly equal to the difference between the inflation numbers of Turkey and of those countries. On the graph, the imaginary horizontal line crossing 100 designates the assumed exchange rate. If the lines are above the 100–line then it means that the Turkish currency has been appreciated or vice versa. For instance, if we look at the lines in February 2001, we can see that TL was 48 percent appreciated with respect to CPI and 18 percent appreciated with respect to WPI — certainly based on the assumption that the exchange rate in 1995 was correct. We know that the foreign trade deficit had increased dramatically, reaching up to 5 percent of GNP, that is, US $9.8 billion during this period.

b. By June 2004, it seems that the TL has appreciated by 28 percent and 38 percent with respect to WPI and CPI respectively (based on the 1 + 0.77 Euro exchange basket).

c. We know that the value of the TL is closely linked to foreign trade, and that particularly, the appreciated TL combined with the increase in the domestic demand will substantially increase imports. It has also a negative influence on exports, but the influence on imports is more indicative. However, this relation must be explained by taking the costs into the consideration.

d. Let us call attention to research carried out for the ready-made clothing sector which constitutes the "engine" of the exports (30 percent of the total industrial products export). The cost (thread and fabric prices) which shows the worsening competitive environment, and the exchange rate index are demonstrated in the table below. It is obvious that the increase in the costs has been exceeding the increase in the exchange rate from the second half of 2001. On the other hand, the labor costs which constitute 30 percent of the production costs have increased by 40 percent at the beginning of 2004. When we consider that the unit export prices have been decreasing as a result of intense competition in the world, we have to worry about the sector which "bears" 30 percent of both the industrial goods exports and the employment.

Table 14. The Developments in the Ready-Made Clothing Sector (based on the costs and the exchange rate index)

Period	Cost Index	Euro Index	Dollar Index
2000 1st half	100	100	100
2000 2nd half	116.3	104.3	112.9
2001 1st half	158.1	156.8	168.6
2001 2nd half	226.1	231.6	248.7
2002 1st half	256.9	220.8	235.7
2002 2nd half	290.8	287.3	277.8
2003 1st half	320.6	309.4	269.2
2003 2nd half	337.8	290.9	241.1
2004 1st half	354.6	303.1	236.9

SOURCE: ITKIB JULY 2004 "HAZIRGIYIM VE KONFEKSIYON SEKTÖRÜNÜN 2004 OCAK-HAZIRAN IHRACAT PERFORMANS DEĞERLENDIRMESI"

e. Recently, the private sector often mentions that the positive influence of the increasing productivity on competitiveness has been reduced due to the increasing costs, leading to a decline in the profit margins. In exports, especially in the sectors which have high value added and significant contribution to employment, the narrowing margins are noticeable. On the other hand, the automotive industry which has had an important role in the recent increase in exports (this sector has a relatively low added value; for a US $100 export, a US $75 imports is needed) is also experiencing this narrowing margin problem. However, the profit constitutes the propelling force for the new investments which would create new employment areas. Having problems in making profit, the sector has been left with no option, but to increase productivity. However, increasing costs (labor, tax, energy, and other raw materials) wipe away the profits which have been earned as a result of the increased productivity. For this reason, the level of the exchange rate becomes important here.

How Does the Float Work?

How are the exchange rates determined in the floating regimes? Are there any factors other than the Central Bank that affect the exchange rate?

In fact, it is very difficult to estimate the exchange rate in the floating regimes. Still, you can calculate what it must be. This calculation is done by the Purchasing Power Parity approach.

For instance, at the beginning of 2002, US $1 was approximately equal to 1 million 430 thousand Turkish Liras. Inflation in Turkey was 30 percent in the same year, whereas it was 2 percent in the USA. Given these circumstances, according to the above method at the end of the year, US $1 must have been equal to 1 million 822 thousand Turkish Liras. Yet it was 1 million 630 thousand.

You can disagree with this calculation. You can say that the Euro gained 5.5 percent value against US $1 in 2002. And that's true...

Then when you remove this effect, it would not have been below 1 million 700 thousand. On the other hand, you may question whether the 1 million 430 thousand was the correct rate. Right... The correct rate at the end of 2002 must have been higher...

Our scope here is not to discuss the reasons for this, but to analyze the determinations of the exchange rates in the floating regimes... Now, let's get to the second point...

Relative interest rate differences between the two currencies also influence the exchange rates. For instance, if the interest rate for the Euro is 3.5 percent while it is 1.5 percent for the US dollar then market agents take place in action...

The speculators, who have borrowed the dollar at a 1.5 percent cost, convert it to Euro in order to get 3.5 percent interest revenue. Thus, the Euro can appreciate against the dollar in a market where there is demand for the Euro and supply for the dollar...

The other economic factors determining the exchange rates are related to the economic performance of the countries... Macroeconomic factors such as growth rate, unemployment rate, taxes, balance of payments including exports and imports, public sector debts, public sector deficits and sustainability of these, inflation, real interest rates and so on, play a role in determining the value of the country's currency...

In the floating exchange rate regime, along with the three economic factors that we have listed here, non-economic factors like the political structure and social behavior may also affect the exchange rates...

f. We do not see any necessity to mention the importance of the competitive power in keeping the foreign trade deficit under control, again. Nevertheless, it is also important to take claims such as the exchange rate regime in Turkey is "free floating and the exchange rates are determined by the supply and demand balance in the market" into consideration. First, let us explore the main characteristics, advantages and disadvantages of the floating exchange rate regime in the table below.

Table 15. Advantages and Disadvantages of the Floating Exchange Rate Regime

Advantages	Disadvantages
• Provides resistance to external/real shocks. • Provides competitive power in foreign trade. • Allows implementation of independent fiscal policy (Central Bank involved in determining the short term interest rates only).	• Inflation import. • Reduced trade and fiscal activity because of the increased risks. • Damage in the real and the fiscal sector caused by the exchange rate risk.

g. Turkey yielded US $14 billion foreign trade deficit and US $6.8 billion current account trade deficit in 2003. While the total current account deficit in the first five months of 2004 was US $8.4 billion, the foreign trade deficit of the first half of the year reached US $16.8 billion. According to the recommendation of the Central Bank, considering the difficulties of calculating the foreign suitcase trade, the current account deficit should not be perceived as "alarming".

h. The most important advantage of the floating exchange rate regime is to provide competitive power in foreign trade. However, in spite of the "shocking" developments of 2004, an appreciating Turkish Lira does not conform to the system's basics. The exchange rate must respond to this level of deficit, but for some reason (!) this response never appears. We see that the position of the institutions and expectation management have an influence on this to a great extent. For instance, the Central Bank has announced that "the only buyer of the exchange is the bank itself" between March 2003 and March 2004, but the balance sheet of the bank does not verify this. The Central Bank if necessary intervenes in the markets and purchases foreign exchange, but at the same time keeps selling foreign exchange, too

Central Bank and the Foreign Exchange Rates

Another discussion on foreign exchange relates to how much the Central Bank purchases foreign exchange. As we know, the Central Bank can purchase foreign exchange in the market both directly and through the tender method. Nowadays, it has announced that it would buy maximum US $80 million by daily tenders. In addition, it has purchased a sizeable amount of foreign exchange (slightly over US $1 billion) by intervening in the market in the last one-month period.

The President of the Central Bank often announces that "there is no other foreign exchange purchaser, but the bank." Moreover, he indicates that the Central Bank has already purchased approximately US $8–9 billion.

These kinds of explanations are naturally perceived differently by the public. The firms, first of all the banks, the finance houses and individual investors naturally think: "As nobody is purchasing foreign exchange, why should we? On the contrary, we should also sell our foreign exchange and utilize the high TL revenue".

Let us come to the US $8–9 billion foreign exchange purchase of the Central Bank, which the President often mentions. If the Central Bank is purchasing foreign exchange, we should see it in the balance sheet of the bank. The difference between the Bank's foreign exchange assets and liabilities indicates the Bank's Net Exchange Reserve. Based on this fact, we can calculate the "net" foreign exchange amount. The table below shows the development of the Bank's Net Exchange Position:

CENTRAL BANK'S NET FOREIGN EXCHANGE POSITION (US $ MILLION)

March 28, 2003	- 911
October 31, 2003	2,689
December 26, 2003	54
February 13, 2004	1,191

On March 28, 2003, the date that we can take as the end of the war during the USA occupation of Iraq, the difference between the Bank's foreign exchange assets and liabilities, which indicates the Bank's Net Foreign Exchange Position was yielding US $911 million deficit. In other words, the Bank's foreign exchange assets were less than its foreign exchange liabilities. This shows that the bank yielded US $911 million short position.

However, with the end of the war and as a result of the returning of the outflowed foreign exchange into the system, workers' remittances and tourism revenues in the summer, the foreign exchange supply increased. All these factors when combined with the Bank's foreign exchange purchases allow the bank to cover its short position and to yield a US $2 billion 689 million foreign exchange surplus. In short, the Central Bank closed its US $911 million short position by purchasing foreign exchange. Thus, we can calculate how much foreign exchange the bank purchased between March and October and it was US $3 billion 600 million.

However, we observe that the Bank sold US $2 billion 635 million between October and December because the Bank's net foreign exchange surplus was reduced to US $54 million at the end of December.

According to the latest balance sheet dated February 13, 2004, of the Central Bank, the net foreign exchange surplus was US $1 billion 191 million. This shows that the bank has bought net US $1 billion 137 million from the new year to February 13.

To sum up, the Central Bank purchased US $2 billion 102 million foreign exchange between March 2003 when the war ended and February 13, 2004. Thus, we have determined the net amount of the foreign exchange that the Bank purchased.

Consequently, we can question the argument of the Bank about the purchase of over US $10 billion. While indicating the amount of the foreign exchange it has purchased, the Bank does not say anything about its foreign exchange sales or the decrease in its assets. This leads the market to misperception.

Briefly, the Central Bank is successful in expectation management.

We have to observe that the amount which keeps the foreign exchange rate in its low level is around US $2.6 billion. Who do you think is benefiting from the appreciation of TL resulting from foreign support and psychological reasons to a great extent?

i. The appreciation of TL primarily suits the interest of the Treasury who converted the TL instruments in the banks' assets to foreign currency-indexed instruments, and who exported foreign exchange and foreign currency-indexed debt instruments in order to stop the foreign exchange demand. Therefore, the Treasury portfolio was exposed to a high foreign exchange rate risk, not only because of the foreign debts, but also because of a portion of the domestic debts which were indexed to foreign currency. If we analyze the situation by May 2004 – the share of the foreign debts was even higher in the previous periods – the US $204 billion debt stock consists of US $63 billion foreign debt and US $141 billion domestic debt. However, approximately US $22 billion of the domestic debts are foreign currency-indexed, in other words, approximately US $85 billion of the total Treasury debts are either foreign exchange-based or foreign currency-indexed. In spite of this, the Treasury is an institution collecting revenues (taxes) in TL. For this reason, it stands in a serious short position, and an increase in the foreign exchange rate has an immediate negative effect on the Treasury. On the other hand, the borrowing cost of the Treasury decreases with the appreciation of TL. The Treasury, who does not pay high interests for TL borrowings, pays less real interest as long as the foreign exchange rates are low, and thus minimizes its borrowing cost on the average. This can be observed in the following table. When the real interest burden of the foreign debt is taken into consideration, it is obvious that the decreasing foreign exchange rates have positive effects on the borrowings of the Treasury.

Table 16. Real Interest Burden of the Domestic Debts

	April 2004	Mar 2004	Feb 2004	Jan 2004	Dec 2003
TOTAL	12.33	11.34	11.21	11.39	11.91
PUBLIC	8.22	7.33	7.85	6.81	6.53
TL	10.67	9.64	8.50	8.50	7.66
F. EXCHANGE	- 4.61	- 4.59	4.59	- 1.16	1.5
MARKET	15.21	14.18	13.72	14.89	16.45
TL	18.54	18.77	19.39	19.88	22.35
F. EXCHANGE	2.31	- 3.12	- 6.56	- 1.73	- 0.04

SOURCE: TT

j. Another group which will be affected by the exchange rates, is the fiscal sector. We know that the increase in the exchange rates triggers the interest rates. If the interest rates increase, the banking system and the institutions which carry serious amounts of securities (Government Domestic Debt Instruments (GDDI), Eurobonds, other debt instruments, stocks and so on.) in their assets, will be affected. In 2002 and 2003 the share of the securities in the banks' assets is around 40 percent (of course this ratio was higher in 2001). In other words, the banks keep 67 percent of their saving deposits as Government Domestic Debt Instruments (GDDI). This ration increases to 83 percent in the state banks.

k. The large portfolio of GDDI in the fiscal system will encounter the risk of losing its value with the increasing foreign exchange and interest rates. In this case, a deterioration in the assets' structure will be inevitable. On the other hand, the short positions which have been attained through borrowing in foreign exchange and converting it to TL, will endanger the real sector, although the level of the positions are not as high as in 2000.

Table 17. Banks' Assets Structure

	2003 (trillion TL)	2003 % share	2002 % share
LIQUID ASSETS	36,284	14.5	16.2
SECURITIES PORTFOLIO	106,910	42.8	40.5
- Trading securities	30,026	12.0	9.8
- Securities to be sold	30,668	12.2	8.3
- Securities to be kept till maturity	46,217	18.5	22.4
LOANS	74,929	28.0	26.5
- Follow-up loans	8,629	3.4	4.9
- Special reserves	7,641	3.0	3.1
FIXED ASSETS	19,242	7.7	8.5
- Participation share	2,386	1.4	1.4
- Partnership	6,252	2.5	2.5
- Material fixed assets	10,196	4.0	4.5
- Non-material fixed assets	407	0.1	0.2
OTHER ASSETS	17,315	6.9	8.5
TOTAL ASSETS	249,750	100.0	100.0

l. Another consequence of the appreciation of TL is increasing imports and thus, VATs which are collected from the sales of imported goods. The taxes imposed on the imports and the increase in the VAT in some sectors as a result of the increasing domestic demand have been of great help to the Ministry of Finance which has had a hard time to collect taxes in the first half of 2004 in spite of the economic growth.

m. The growth which started with the appreciation of the Turkish currency, and which was obtained by the stimulation of domestic demand by the consumer credits in some sectors (automotive and so on.) has been found to be successful by the IMF, (August 1, 2001 Sunday, *Hürriyet* Newspaper, IMF Mission Chief in Turkey Riza Moghadam p. 8) but some preventive measures must be taken to keep the current account deficit under control. Without a doubt, this brings the necessity of reducing domestic demand: tighter budget, more primary surplus, price increases in SEE products and cooling of the economy…

n. It seems not possible to prevent the appreciation of the TL because of the borrowing structure and costs of the Treasury, and the portfolios of the fiscal institutions. In other words, the Treasury would do anything to prevent the use of the foreign exchange rate "weapon" for increasing the competitive power of Turkey. However, the steps toward a decrease in domestic demand and the target of closing the current account deficit will obviously reduce the tax revenues that are collected from imports and domestic consumption. As a conclusion, we expect that the appreciated TL will have a negative effect on the competitive power and the current account deficit will inevitably continue in an environment where the costs are not and/or cannot be reduced (for instance, the Social Security Institution's premium burden cannot be reduced because of the deficit in the social security system, taxes cannot be decreased, energy costs are still high…)

o. The position of the fiscal institutions and the Treasury makes us think once more about whether the exchange rate regime in Turkey is "floating" or not. It is obvious that the Central Bank will not want inflation to rise again as a result of the uncertainty caused by the floating regime and the potential increase in the exchange rates. For this reason, even though "the Bank sometimes gives appropriate warnings", it must admit that the basic problems cannot be overcome with the appreciated TL and expectation management, and that the "breathing operation" which was provided by keeping the TL appreciated cannot be sustained and cannot eliminate the vulnerability of the economy.

4.7 Long-term domestic and foreign debts must be found and costs must be decreased

One of the most important problems of Turkey is the cost and the maturity of her domestic and foreign debts. As the IMF delegation often say, Turkey is paying the highest real interest in the world with Brazil. We have analyzed the cost of the domestic and foreign debts in detail in the previous section. Here, we would like to highlight that Turkey is implementing appreciated TL policy in order to decrease the cost of her borrowing. With the appreciated TL, costs are controlled since most of the debts are either foreign exchange-based or foreign exchange-indexed. On the other hand, this situation brings a lot of problems related to the current account deficit. Since we have already discussed the reasons why Turkey pays high real interest in the previous section, we will not go into details here.

On the other hand, the maturity of the debts which is due within two years, constitutes another basic problem. Short terms make it very difficult to sustain the debts in the fiscal markets which are already too shallow. Certainly, this also causes an increase in the real interest rates. The same problem will be encountered with foreign borrowing if the new program with the IMF is not implemented. Starting from 2005, Turkey will have to repay all her debts in three years. There is no need to discuss that while yielding the current account deficit it will be too difficult to be able to pay for net foreign debt. In a period when Turkey yields current account deficit, there is no need to say that she faces difficulties in repaying net foreign debt.

It is not possible to extend terms by just offering higher interest rates to long terms. First of all, the depositors must have confidence in the financial markets, and must be convinced that the macroeconomic stability has been achieved.

4.8 There must be a net positive primary surplus in a stable growing economy without restricting social needs

Primary surplus is a critical concept in the sustainability of the public sector debts. There is an important relationship between the primary surplus and the reduction of the ratio of the public sector debt to the gross national income under 60 percent which is an EU criterion. The public sector yielding a primary surplus of 6.5 percent of the national income will not only reduce this ratio, but also ease the sustainability of the debts.

However, we should mention a basic assumption here: it is

not possible to reduce the ratio of the public debt to the national income by just yielding primary surplus and by economic growth. If the burden of the real interest exceeds these two critical ratios (primary surplus and economic growth), again it will be impossible to reduce the debt ratio. Therefore, real interest rates must be declined roughly below the sum of the economic growth and the primary surplus.

WHY IS THE DOMESTIC DEBT INCREASING WHILE THE INTEREST RATES ARE DECREASING?

At the beginning of the 2000 stabilization program, there were two main targets: to reduce inflation and to decrease the public debt stock which had already reached 60 percent of the national income, below the EU criterion ratio 60 percent…

The succeeding crises caused significant deviations from the targets. The national income declined substantially while the debt was increasing. A partial recovery was observed in 2002. In 2003, the political stability and "the obligatory hope" created by the positions taken, provided a decrease in the foreign exchange rates. With this relief, all the indicators which were calculated on the TL basis, were inflated on the dollar basis. The National Income was increasing rapidly on dollar basis. As a result of net primary surplus and fiscal discipline, debt stock was brought under control. Finally, the sustainability of the debts was no longer a problem.

As we know, the public sector's (only the Treasury's excluding the Central Bank's) foreign and domestic debt stock consists of 55 percent of TL and 45 percent of foreign exchange and foreign exchange-indexed debts by February 2004. The downward trend in the foreign exchange raises the TL portion of the debt stock if converted to foreign exchange. As a result, with the trend of the exchange rate in 2003, we can say that the TL portion of the debt stock has increased by approximately 10 percent on the dollar basis. However, when it comes to the calculation of the real interest payments the reverse is observed. As a result of the negative trend in the exchange rates, the real interest burden of the foreign exchange-based and foreign exchange-indexed debts which constitute 50 percent of the total debt stock, was turned to negative by 15 percent. This means, the foreign exchange debt which is around half of the total debts, has a negative real interest burden. The negative "snowball" effect of this on the debt stock should not be forgotten…

Another development which has an impact on the debt stock is the burden of the Imar Bank which is approximately TL 10 quadrillion. This equals 2 percent of the national income. The markets have not even considered this burden. Anyway, this is not the subject of our discussion…

To sum up, let us look at the developments in the debt stock: by the end of 2002 the total foreign and domestic capital debt stock was around US $148 billion. The public sector debt stock increased by 36 percent on the dollar basis and reached US $202.7 billion. Hence, the ratio of the public sector debt to the national income could not be reduced below 70 percent as targeted. On the contrary, it increased up to 84 percent. We may assume that 10 percent of this was due to the exchange rate and Imar Bank. Yet, the final ratio was too high. In addition, if we consider the negative trend in the exchange rates turning the real interest burden to negative, we can observe that the ratio of the public debt stock to the national income is even higher than it was in 2002. We would like to remind the reader that the foreign debts of the Central Bank and private sector have not been included in these figures…

All right, then what are we discussing while the debt stock is expanding like a snowball?

Nowadays, the news about the increase of the domestic debt stock in spite of the declining interest rates is perceived to be contradictory. If the interests are declining why is the debt increasing? Let us analyze these figures:

1. The TL 36.4 quadrillion domestic debt stock in 2000 increased to TL 122.2 quadrillion in 2001, TL 149.9 quadrillion in 2002 and TL 194.4 quadrillion in 2003. By the end of May 2004 the stock has reached to TL 209 quadrillion.

2. The main problem in Turkey is to reduce the domestic debt and at the same time the ratio of the public sector's total debt stock to the National Income. Otherwise, the absolute domestic debt stock cannot be reduced; on the contrary it will continue to increase each month. Certainly, if the government decides to meet the budget deficits by only foreign debt from now on, then the capital domestic debt stock will remain the same. However, in that case, foreign debt will increase as much as the budget deficit. Shortly, without a surplus in Turkey's public sector budget, it is not possible to decrease the

capital amount of the domestic and foreign debt stocks. And as there will not be a budgetary surplus (!), the debt stock will continue to increase. In other words, the Treasury will borrow for both the foreign and the domestic debt stocks as well as for the budget deficit...

3. Now, what can be done to reduce this ratio? The answer lies in the ratio itself: in order to increase the National Income, sustainable growth must be achieved in the economy. On the other hand, the primary surplus must be yielded as much as possible (IMF's primary surplus target is 6.5 percent).

4. Let us explain this primary surplus concept a little bit more: For instance, in 2004 the target for the Consolidated Budget Revenues is TL 114.5 quadrillion. If we were not to pay for the interests of foreign and domestic debts, the non-interest expenditures would be TL 94.7 quadrillion. Under these circumstances, (114.5 minus 94.7) the budget would yield TL 19.8 quadrillion. This number designates the primary surplus. However, we have to pay TL 66.2 quadrillion interest for the domestic and foreign debts...

Now appears the role of the primary surplus: we can cover TL 19.8 quadrillion of interest payments by the budget revenues. Then if TL 19.8 quadrillion primary surplus is subtracted from TL 66.2 interest payments, the remainder is TL 46.4 quadrillion which is the budget deficit of 2004. The Treasury will borrow then an amount equal to the total of both the capital of the domestic and foreign debts and the budget deficit (TL 46.4 quadrillion) interest. This proves that the absolute debts of Turkey will continue to increase.

5. After explaining the importance of the primary surplus explicitly, we must now point to another fact. For instance, the target set for the ratio of the public sector primary surplus to the national income is 6.5 percent for 2004. Furthermore, the estimated economic growth is 5 percent. Under these circumstances, is it possible to reduce the ratio of the public sector debt to the national income? The answer is maybe...

6. It is not enough to meet these two targets. Roughly speaking, the level of the Treasury's borrowing interest is also important. If the real interest rates cannot be pulled roughly below the total of the primary surplus and the economic growth, the indebtedness may increase again…

7. As inflation decreases, the interest rates also decrease, but this decreasing interest rate is the nominal interest rate. The decrease in the real interest rates is as important as that in the nominal interest rates. We know that the Treasury borrowed at 24.4 percent nominal interest rate in January-February period of this year. The WPI shows 9.1 percent inflation. Given these circumstances, the real interest rate remains around 14 percent. This ratio was 14.5 percent for 2003 and 6.5 percent for 2002. For 2004 the real interest burden of the domestic debt is 14 percent. This is more than the total of the primary surplus and the growth…

8. Therefore, we can say that the indebtedness ratio cannot be reduced. But the fact is that the domestic debt stock is equivalent to approximately 70 percent of the total public debt stock. And some portion of it is indexed to foreign currency. The remaining 30 percent constitutes the foreign debt. We can follow this from the table below…

9. The real interest burden of the TL portion of the domestic debt is 14 percent but the burden of foreign exchange-indexed debt is negative. Then, the real interest burden of the total debts remains under the total of the primary surplus and the growth. This decreases the indebtedness ratio while making the sustainability of the debts easier.

10. We have to consider this fact when we discuss the level of the exchange rates in the markets. The Treasury continues its policy characterized by its will to support the rate or its "reluctant" pursuit of appreciated TL. We know that the markets or at least the market agents know this fact.

Finally, the debt stock will continue to increase, even though the interest rates are decreasing. However, in order to sustain the debts, the exchange rate must not increase…

Table 18. Treasury Domestic and Foreign Debt Stock
(US $ billion)

	May 2004	2002	2003	Ratio to GNP 2002	Ratio to GNP 2003
Domestic Debt	141.3	91.7	139.3	50.5	58.5
Public	57.5	48.4	66.4	26.6	27.9
Market	83.7	43.3	72.9	23.8	30.6
Foreign Debt	63.0	56.8	63.4	31.3	26.6
Credit	36.5	33.7	36.6	18.5	15.4
IMF	17.0	13.9	16.7	7.6	7.0
Bond	26.5	23.1	26.8	12.7	11.3
TOTAL	204.3	148.5	202.7	81.7	85.1

SOURCE: TT

If the 6.5 percent primary surplus which was calculated on the date of 2002 and set as a performance criterion by the IMF based on the data of 2002, can be yielded until 2007, the ratio of the public debt will be reduced below 60 percent of the National Income. The maturity problem must be taken into account here, too. Short-term domestic borrowing is an important factor in increasing real interest rates. Without a doubt, there are a lot of factors which affect the real interest, but let us show how the primary surplus is calculated:

Table 19. Consolidated Budget and Primary Surplus
(TL trillion)

	2003 Realized	2004 Program
REVENUES	100,238	104,109
NON-INTEREST EXPENDITURE	- 81,444	83,895
PRIMARY SURPLUS	18,794	20,214
INTEREST PAYMENTS	- 58,609	66,050
BUDGET DEFICIT	- 39,815	- 45,836
GNP	357,045	419,692
Consolidated Budget Primary Surplus/GNP	5.3	4.8

SOURCE: TT

The IMF's target for the ratio, which is also known as Public Total Main Surplus, is 6.5 percent. Yet, as we can see from the table above, 4.8 percent of 6.5 percent for instance in 2004 will be met from the consolidated budget. The rest will then be transferred to the budget by 25 SEEs and 3 funds, for the interest payments.

There is no doubt that one of the most important provisions of the arrangement with the IMF, will be the primary surplus. For this reason, it is possible that there may be some problems between the economy administration and the IMF, since the main target of the economy administration is to decrease interest rates and control inflation. However, the IMF's priority will be the primary surplus because it believes that the only condition to sustain the debts and reduce the real interest rates is to yield a primary surplus. This ties the hands of the economy administration to make expenditures. It seems that the unemployment which is the natural consequence of insufficient profitability and lack of investments, will compel the economy administration in the following period. As the targets of the economy administration and IMF do not overlap, the main problems of the Turkish economy continue to deepen: the economy is growing but it is not perceived by a wide section of society (unemployment increases), the inflation is declining but society does not perceive it, a growth is realized due to the appreciation of TL, the approach in the sustainability of debts is not reflected on the operational revenues of the real sector, and the Ministry of Finance cannot increase its tax revenues. It is a recovery which is "peculiar", bearing many doubts about its sustainability...

To sum up, the primary surplus is the essence of the stabilization program. However, it is obvious that it is putting pressure on the social equilibrium. On the other hand, SEEs need to increase prices in order to meet the targets. This also contradicts with the inflation target...

CONCLUSION

Conditions for the success of a new program with the IMF

Achieving single-digit inflation rates, increasing industrial capacity utilization up to the limits along with serious improvements in productivity, the Turkish economy seems to have overcome the crisis of 2001. Beyond all doubt, in order to sustain this situation and to inspire confidence in both the domestic and foreign investors, these developments should be permanent and the uncertainties about the future should be eliminated.

In the previous section, we have discussed the conditions for the success of Turkey's current program with the IMF and the one which will be implemented from the beginning of 2005. In order to sustain the current "positive" development in Turkish economy, all of the provisions must be simultaneously met. If any trouble takes place in performing one and/or more of these, new crises will inevitably be undergone in the future. For this reason, in order to discuss the future of the Turkish economy in the short run and the sustainability of the stability that Turkey "seems" to have attained, it is necessary to go over the developments both at home and in the world, and determine the effects of these developments (as mentioned in the box below) on the conditions of success.

FOREIGN CONJUNCTURE AND TURKEY'S NEED FOR FOREIGN FINANCE

a. First, let us point to the international developments: The United States Economy Administration has pulled down the short-term interest rates to the 1 percent level for the first time in 50 years, and applied massive tax cuts in order to come out of the recession of 2001. The decline of the short-term interest rates down to 1 percent led the institutions to take short-term loans and then purchase long-term bonds and/or securities because the institutions were racing to get the most benefit from the differences in the short- and long-term interest rates. The general decline in the interest rates did not only revive the securities market, but also the real estate market. Massive tax cuts of the Bush Administration combined with the robust budget deficits and decline in the interest rates revitalized the economy, and consequently inflationist trends started to emerge. Inflation data of the USA pointed up to 3 percent.

b. US $500 billion of budget deficit and the equal amount of trade deficit of the USA are called "twin deficits" and is a world record. Under these circumstances, FED has nothing to do but inevitably raise the interest rates gradually. FED has shown signs of future increases in the market while it was increasing the rates by 0.25 percent (by the time the study was prepared FED had increased the interest rates to 1.25 percent). Everyone agrees that it is inevitable to raise the interest rates but the question here is whether FED will wait for the American Presidential elections in November or increase the interest rates in the shorter run. Another issue is the amount of steps and the rates of the increases. Will the interest rates remain around 3.5 percent within the next 2 years or will they rise up to around 6.5 percent again? On the other hand, will the increase in the United States' interest rates trigger the same trend in other countries?

c. It is important to note here that FED acts with deliberation in increasing the interest rates. By making announcements about the interest rates such as "the increase is possible," FED warns the institutional investors to be careful. There is a fear behind all these deliberate acts: possible high volume sales of securities (bonds, stocks and so on.) and real estates due to the expectation of a raise in the interest rates. If the investors expect that the securities and real estates will lose value due to an increase in the interest rates, they will sell them. FED's moderate attempts are now accepted in the financial markets because the USA has no ability to cope with a financial crisis especially under the current circumstances in the Middle East.

Nor does any other country. However, despite all these deliberate moves FED's attempt to increase the interest rates has already started to affect the developing countries such as Turkey.

d. Similar reflections have appeared on the Eurobonds of the developing countries. Beginning with Brazil all bonds of the countries have been sold, naturally including those of Turkey. Without any change in the credibility note of Turkey, the revenues of the Eurobond have reached the 10 percent level from 8 percent as a result of the increase by 0.25 percent by FED. Of course, the developments have not been limited to the Eurobonds. The interest rates of the Government Domestic Debt Instruments (GDDI) have also increased, resulting in voluminous sales and increase in the foreign exchange rates by over 15 percent, that is, the TL depreciated in April 2004. Thus, the increase signal in the USA interest rates and expectations about its sustainability did not only reflect on the Eurobonds, but also on the borrowing costs. From now on, the level of these costs will be dependent upon the FED's decisions for the level of the interest rates. Within this framework, we encounter another question: will the results of the increase in the interest rates in the USA be limited to the increase in the borrowing costs or will they involve other problems in finding foreign finance?

e. Another problem which is affecting the world economy is the price of oil which currently fluctuates within US $35–40 band. The oil prices are highly susceptible to the increases in the world oil demand, primarily the increase of the consumption of China. On the other hand, being the target of global terrorism, the oil pipelines and the employees of this industry constitute another pressure on the prices. The markets are familiar with the US $35–50 band. The increase in the oil prices does not only increase the costs, but also causes a flow of the funds from oil dependent countries such as Turkey to the oil exporting countries. We know that the cost of oil for Turkey has increased by around US $1.4 billion.

f. Another problem in the world economy is the growth rate

reaching 9 percent primarily in China and the dramatic increase in the raw material prices due to developments in the world demand. This pressure on the prices is threatening the costs and consequently the inflation targets of the countries. For the time being, Turkey does not feel this price pressure because of the overvalued TL. However, this must be anticipated as a threat.

CURRENT DEVELOPMENTS IN THE TURKISH ECONOMY

g. After the analysis of the international environment, we should evaluate the circumstances and the developments in Turkey. We must admit that Turkey has proceeded in increasing productivity and output after the 2001 crisis. The increases in the GNP in 2002 and 2003 by 7.9 and 5.9 percent respectively were originating from foreign demand, in other words from exports. On the other hand, the movements in domestic demand appeared in 2003, but in a limited number of sectors such as automotive and durable goods sectors. However, the domestic demand boom in the final quarter of 2003 which was triggered by the low consumer credits shows that domestic demand has replaced exports within the growth. While the agricultural sector received a blow (with a negative growth rate in the first quarters of 2001, 2003 and 2004) the construction sector moved forward in the first quarter of 2004. Due to the sales campaigns and the consumer credits, future income is spent in the present particularly for motor vehicles and durables. On the other hand, private sector investments which are revived as a result of decreasing interest and exchange rates constitute another component of the domestic demand. The growth based on the domestic demand causes a dramatic increase in the imports, and consequently a widening trade deficit becomes inevitable. And this leads to the current account deficit which is attempted to be covered with hot money and short-term capital movements. It should be noted that the media continuously makes mention of the success in exports and never talks about the boom in imports and as a result the current account deficit. The details of the foreign trade developments and the risks involved are discussed in the box below.

THE ANALYSIS OF FOREIGN TRADE AND ITS EFFECTS ON THE FOREIGN EXCHANGE RATE

The foreign trade figures have been announced by the State Institute of Statistics. According to this data: in May 2004, exports increased by 23.4 percent compared to the figures of May 2003 and reached US $4.8 billion while imports in the same period increased by 44.1 percent reaching US $8 billion. This increase in imports caused the foreign trade deficit to widen increasing to US $3.2 billion in May 2004 from US $1.7 billion in May 2003. In the first five months of the year compared to the same period of 2003, exports increased by 29.3 percent reaching US $23.1 billion, and imports increased by 47.2 percent reaching US $37 billion. The US $7.2 billion foreign trade deficit of 2003 Jan-May term increased by 91.6 percent and reached US $13.8 billion in the same period of 2004.

DETAILS OF FOREIGN TRADE:

1. When we elaborate the export data, we can see that 95 percent of the total increase stems from the exports of the manufacture industry goods. Particularly, an increase in the exports of the automotive and by-product industries is obvious. The data of the first five months of this year also proves this. The other two sectors which have contributed to exports are the iron-steel and electric appliances industries.

2. The exports to Iraq also contributed to the increase. The total export to Iraq in the first five months reached US $600 million. Thus, Iraq rose to the tenth position among the countries to which Turkey exports most. Furthermore, exports to the major markets such as England, France and Spain increased substantially by about 40 to 45 percent. Another important observation about the first five months is the 83 percent increase in the exports to the United Arab

Graph 11. Monthly Export and Import (in US $ billion)

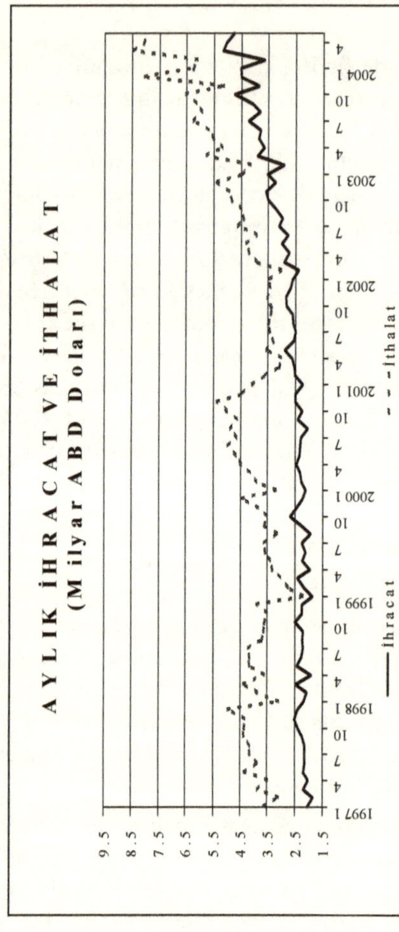

NOTE: THE SOLID LINE INDICATES EXPORT, AND THE DOTTED LINE IMPORT.

Emirates which takes the eighth position. To sum up, Iraq and the United Arab Emirates are the developing export markets for Turkey.

3. When we elaborate the imports data, we see a substantial increase by 180 percent in the motor vehicles imports in May as we have already observed in the exports. Even though the intermediate goods imports increased by 31 percent in Jan-May period of 2004, both the increase in the consumer goods and capital goods imports were much more influential in the total overall 47 percent increase in the imports.

4. The rising crude oil prices played an important role in the increasing imports. In May, the crude oil imports were increased by 50 percent.

5. While the export coverage rate was around 70 percent in Jan-May of 2003, it reduced to 62 percent in the same period in 2004. Further reduction to 59 percent in May must be anticipated as a serious threat because usually, 60 percent export coverage rate is regarded as a critical value.

6. We may argue that the increase in the imports is related to growth. While the production is dependent on the foreign countries, it is reasonable to think that growth can increase the imports. However, we should note the effect of the exchange rate here. We know that it is possible to import many commodity inputs at cheaper prices (compared to the local prices; for instance, granite as an intermediate good; Baghdad Street has been paved with granite stones imported from China; our granite unfortunately cannot compete with the Chinese on a price basis) in the international markets since the TL is appreciated. Thus, we know that growth has the most important effect on imports, but we must accept the fact that the TL is appreciated.

7. Another opinion is that the increase in exports is related to the increase in the automotive production; however, the highest increase was observed in the exports of this sector. On the other hand, this sector is at the same time dependent upon the imports (appr. 75 percent), which brings the problem of its added value. In brief, exports are increasing but the biggest

increase is in the import-dependent exports which do not bring much value added to the country. The export margins continue to narrow down based on research conducted by Turkish Exporters Assembly (TIM). Yet, we must keep in mind what encourages the private sector investments and that employment is the profit.

Table 20. Foreign Trade in terms of Commodity Categories

(million dollar)	May '03	May '04	Jan–May '03	Jan–May '04	May change	Jan–May change
Exports	3,680	4,763	17,888	23,123	23.4%	29.3%
Capital goods	315	472	1,667	2,206	50.0%	32.4%
Intermediate goods	1,629	2,038	7,408	9,373	25.1%	26.5%
Consumption goods	1,869	2,241	8,709	11,485	19.9%	31.9%
Others	47	12	104	59	-73.7%	-43.7%
Imports	5,532	7,970	25,110	36,958	44.1%	47.2%
Capital goods	927	1,572	3,559	6,690	69.6%	88.0%
Intermediate goods	3,961	5,070	18,918	24,841	28.0%	31.3%
Consumption goods	612	1,307	2,481	5,222	113.6%	110.5%
Others	32	21	152	205	-32.9%	35.2%
Foreign trade deficit	-1,671	-3,207	-7,222	-13,835	91.8%	91.6%

SOURCE: SIS

8. The overvalued TL and high input costs constitute a serious problem in exports which has been compensated so far by the appreciation of the Euro against the dollar and by the increased productivity. If we look at the export price index and parity comparison below, we can see that the export prices are increasing. However, this conclusion is misleading because export prices are evaluated on dollar basis, whereas 55 percent of the exports are done on a Euro basis. But the results are based on the dollar.

9. The increase in the import prices points to the increase in the oil and the commodity prices. This is a serious problem. The crude oil prices increased up to US $41 and the depreciation

178

of the dollar along with the increasing commodity prices continue to threaten the cost structures of the dependent countries such as Turkey.

10. On the other hand, it is possible that the increasing imports can affect growth in a positive direction by means of the increasing import tax which constitutes one of the most important revenues of the Turkish economy. While the motor vehicle imports increased as a result of the use of consumer credits, the public sector revenues increased as well due to consumer credits. The import tax and the VAT which were collected domestically constituted the most important items in the increasing tax revenues.

11. The VAT which was imposed on the imports is around US $1 billion in June, demonstrating that the imports will exceed US $8.5 billion. This raises concerns about the prolonged current deficit. Despite the measures, imports continue to increase.

12. The Foreign Trade Limit Table shows us that the increase in the export prices was less than the increase in the import prices, if the effect of the exchange rate is eliminated (as the graph approaches to 100 the prices of the imports and the exports increase at the same rates). We should certainly take into account the effect of the strong Euro in the increase in the export prices.

SHORT NOTES ON THE FOREIGN TRADE AND RESULTS

- We can expect that the US $13.8 billion trade deficit of the five months will reach US $30 billion by the end of the year under these conditions.

- On the other hand, even though the increasing tourism revenues between March and June period (44 percent increase compared to the previous year) will help compensate the foreign trade deficit, the current account trade balance deficit which is based on the foreign exchange inputs and outputs due to the movement of goods and services will be constrained.

- It is obvious that the US $8.8 billion current account deficit of the Jan-May period will continue to expand in May and in

June. The primary fear is the current account deficit exceeding 5 percent of the national income which means a deficit over US $13 billion. The current developments show that the deficit will reach this dangerous level if the growth and the overvaluation of the TL continue.

- For the time being, this deficit is being covered by the short-term capital movements. We cannot talk about foreign direct investment which means a stable foreign exchange input. We must remember that the current deficit which is financed by hot money constitutes a highly vulnerable equilibrium.

- Another strange result is the continuation of the appreciation of TL in a country yielding a substantial foreign exchange deficit and at the same time implementing a floating exchange rate regime. It is important to note that it is not possible to sustain the current situation by hot money.

- For this reason, the EU is used as a magnet to attract foreign investments. However, the necessary conditions for foreign investment to come are an improvement in the investment environment and a reduction in the costs. Since these two cannot be provided what else can be done?

h. On the other hand, we see that relative success has been attained in reducing inflation down to single digits. This success must be permanent though. However, since growth is not reflected on employment, the basic dynamics of the growth process only affects certain parties and town centers. It is clear that the unhealthy growth which reminds us of the year 2000 cannot promote public welfare. The increasing unemployment rates and the productivity increase which cannot be reflected on salaries show that the purchasing power of 2000 has not been reached yet. If the negative trends in agriculture are considered, the attrition of purchasing power combined with the "pressure" on the exchange rate contributes to the decrease in inflation. However, in order to attain a sustainable decrease in inflation, the structural problems must have been solved and the vulnerability must have been eliminated to a great extent.

i.   The IMF European Director Michael Deppler during his visit to Turkey for the eighth Review points to some facts: the most important problem of the Turkish economy is still its public sector debt which is twice as much as the EU member countries, and the real interest rates which are around 15 percent, while they are at most 7 percent in the rest of the world except Brazil.

Table 21. Developments in the Debt Stock

	2002	2003	2004 End of May
Domestic Debt (quadrillion TL)	149.8	194.3	209.0
Total Public Sector Debt (billion US $)	148.5	202.7	204.3
Turkey's Foreign Debt (billion US $)	130.9	147.2	

SOURCE: TT

j.   The developments in the consolidated budget which is made up basically of the domestic and foreign debts of the Treasury are remarkable. Domestic and foreign debt stock which was US $148.5 billion in 2002 increased to US $202.7 billion in 2003, and reached US $204.3 billion by the end of May 2004. Leaving aside the position of the Turkish Lira against the dollar that is, whether its value is realistic or not, we can say that the debt stock continues to increase dramatically. The debts of the Central Bank are not included in this, that is, we only consider here the consolidated budget debt. Nevertheless, we must accept the fact that the ratio of the public sector debt to the National Income has decreased compared to 2001. However, it is still too high for Turkey's conditions. The EU criterion for this ratio is 60 percent maximum. Here, we should ask ourselves if it is enough to take the ratio below 60 percent because compared to the developed financial markets, Turkey's weaker market will always face problems with the rollover of this sizeable debt which continues to be a threat to the Turkish economy. We should note some money supply concepts here. The table below demonstrates the relation between the money supply and the domestic debt in Turkey. In Turkey, the M2 figure comprised of the total of the cash (bills and coins) in our pocket, and both time and demand deposits in TL is around 25 percent of the GNP. However, the ratio of M2 to the GNP is rather high in the other countries: 190 percent in China, 160 percent in Thailand, 100 percent in Israel, 160 percent in South Korea, 85 percent in Indonesia, 70 percent in Hungary, 80 percent in the Czech Republic. If Turkey wants to compare her debt burden and ratio with other countries, she must first compare this structure.

k. Again even if we include the foreign exchange currency deposits, repo deposits and the investment funds in the money supply, still the total will be less than the domestic debts. Especially the short terms of the domestic debts (for example, in 2004 the Treasury projects to pay TL 175 quadrillion of capital and interest payments to the domestic market) and the money supply and/or financial assets being too low create serious problems and increase the real interest burden in the economy trying to manage the debts.

Table 22. Money Supply and the Domestic Debt in Turkey (quadrillion TL)

Money Supply	2004 End of May
M1 = Cash (in the pocket) + TL Demand Deposits	24.0
M2 = M1 + TL Time Deposits	95.1
M2Y = M2 +Foreign Exchange Deposits	164.5
M2YRF = M2Y + Repo + Investment Funds	190.0
Domestic Debt	209.0

SOURCE: CBRT AND TT

l. We must highlight one fact about the public debt: if a couple of negative announcements made by the IMF recently are left aside, we must admit that the IMF support is helpful in the decrease in interest rates. In addition to the easy borrowing especially until March, in the international markets, the IMF's finance support helped to manage the public debts and reduce the costs. In an economy where the budget deficit is about 11 percent of the national income, the state has to borrow in order to manage the current debts and to cover the deficit it has yielded. The problem then, is focused on the composition of the domestic and foreign debts in the total borrowing in a country with a shallow fiscal market such as Turkey. When it is impossible to borrow in the international markets, then the only solution left for the debt rollover is domestic borrowing. With the IMF's support "without reservation" up to now, the administration has not faced a serious difficulty in finding foreign debt. However, the expectation of the interest rate increase in the USA (see the section describing the developments in the world economy) seems to compel the Turkish economy.

m. As we approach the critical period, the most important threat to the program which is based on the sustainability of the public sector debts, will be a possible stagnation in growth. If we compare the realized figures in the first five months of the year (2004) with those of the previous year (2003); 42.1 percent of the expenditure target was realized in the first five months of 2003 whereas this rate remained at just 36 percent in this year. In other words, we remained far below the expenditure target. However, if we divide the expenditures of the consolidated budget into two items as the interest and non-interest expenditures, we observe that last year's figures have remained the same for the latter, whereas there has been a decrease in the former in parallel with the decline in the interest rates. Thus, the reason for falling short of the expenditure target is mainly the decrease in the interest expenditures along with decreasing commodity and service purchases and investments. Given this fact, we may anticipate the increasing interest rates as a sign of increasing interest expenditures in the forthcoming period.

n. On the other hand, if we check the revenues we can observe that the consolidated budget performed well in the first five months in this respect. In the first five months 40.9 percent of the revenues target was realized whereas this rate was 36.7 percent in the first five months of the last year. This is a positive development, but we have to examine it in detail. In May when the corporate and temporary income taxes are collected, we can see a positive increase in the tax revenues due to the fact that the corporates have made high profits in the first quarter of the year. However, tax revenues have a relatively smaller share in the total revenues. Indirect taxes constitute half of the revenues. Oil consumption tax and the import tax have important shares. As long as the growth and imports continue to increase, tax revenues will also increase. However, we should note that tax revenues will be reduced if imports are restricted and if the increase in fuel prices is not reflected on domestic prices. On the other hand, investments and commodity-service purchases which have been postponed to the second half of the year imply that the expenditures will increase in the second half.

o. The ratio of the public sector deficit to the national income is still too high, and the structural reforms cannot be properly realized because the measures do not conform to the realities of the country, and/or there are delays in the implementation. Under these circumstances, we cannot talk about a sustainable recovery of the economy.

p. If we look at similar developments in the fiscal sector, it is obvious that the program is based on the debt rollover. Before the limitation in July of the blanket guarantee protecting bank deposits, the savings in the economy are flowing to the state banks. While the institutional credits are decreasing on real basis, state banks are keeping 84 percent of their TL deposits as government domestic debt instruments. The environment still restricts the fiscal opportunities of the private sector. The relief which is observed in certain sectors because of the consumer credits are not reflected on the real sector completely.

q. The so-called economic growth of over 5 percent has a negative effect on employment. According to the figures of the State Institute of Statistics, the unemployment rate which was

10.2 percent in 2002 increased to 10.5 percent in 2003, and then to 12.4 percent in the first quarter of 2004. Here, it is possible to deduce some facts: the technological investments have decreased employment, while at the same time the employees may not have been registered. However, whatever the reason is, it is not possible to solve the social problems in a country in which 750,000 new people are added each year to the potential employees. Furthermore, we must keep in mind that the economic stability is also affected negatively by this issue.

AS A CONCLUSION

Michael Deppler who is a member of the IMF delegation considers the developments as "extraordinary". He indicates that high public sector debts and a heavy interest burden still threaten the economy, and he points to the fact that the vulnerability is not over yet. The program which has been being implemented for 4 years and which is based on the sacrifice of various parties of society is still carried out by the foreign finance support; unless there is a new arrangement with the IMF in 2005, the so-called debt rollover will no longer be significant, considering the negative developments in the international financial markets. The economy that has become "too dependent" upon foreign finance is a serious problem. The dependence on the IMF and the "powers" behind it is also increasing. Turkey is becoming far from self-sufficient.

In 2005, the Treasury has US $14.5 billion, the Central Bank US $2.9 billion, and the private sector US $7.3 billion foreign debt obligations which are US $26.3 billion in total including the capital and interest payments. The figures for 2006 are similar.

It is inevitable to yield a foreign trade deficit that is, foreign exchange deficit in an economy in which the TL is kept appreciated, the growth is sustained by the consumer credit backed domestic demand and domestic savings cannot be increased. These deficits will certainly be financed with an additional funding. For how long is it possible to reduce these deficits with hot money (high TL interest and low foreign exchange rates) and to manage the public sector debt with foreign borrowing which has become "morphine" for the economy? To what extent will society be able to endure the difficulties and unemployment? How can the competitive power of Turkey be increased as long as the TL is kept appreciated? How can the public sector which yields 11 percent deficit with respect to the national income, decrease the costs (tax, Social Security Institutions premiums, energy and so on.) of the private sector? How can unrecorded economy be prevented with these high costs? How can the real sector manage to pay "by force" for the taxes which cannot be collected from the unrecorded economy? How can the investors be attracted to a country with a low competitive power, high costs and negative investment environment?

All these questions must be clearly answered because the "morale" which is "boosted" by the media – which had been built by international support in a short time – is not sufficient. Now, these hopes must be reflected on real life. The implementations which do not conform with the sustainable growth in a larger part of society may only help in the short term the debt rollover. However, this does not imply that the vulnerability is overcome. The problems are only postponed…

THE CONDITIONS OF SUCCESS OF THE CURRENT PROGRAM AND THE NEW ECONOMIC PROGRAM WHICH WILL BE IMPLEMENTED IN 2005

- The success of the current and the new program which will be implemented in 2005 as a continuation of the current one, is dependent upon the basic assumptions that are listed below. All the parties monitoring the economic developments in Turkey must take these assumptions into consideration in order to see whether the program will be successful or not, and/or to determine the risks involved.

- Turkey should avoid any kind of "stress" that would involve political risks, and achieve a wide range consensus throughout the society.

- Economic relations with the neighboring countries should be improved, expanding joint interests. The position and the function of Turkey in GMEP (Greater Middle East Project) should not involve any risk.
- The structural problems in the world must change in a way that would not stir up any crisis in Turkey. Any kind of economic or political crisis that would cause uncertainty should not take place, a fair competitive environment should be attained and the sustainable growth should continue.
- For a sustainable growth, the structural reforms must be implemented.
- Every year a sizeable (US \$7–8 billion) amount of Foreign Direct Investment must be attracted to the country. And the incoming capital must not only meet the domestic demand but also contribute to export and employment.
- Turkish Lira must not be overvalued.
- Long-term domestic and foreign debts must be found and costs must be decreased.
- There must be a net positive primary surplus in a stable growing economy without restricting social needs.

In order to discuss the future of the economic program, we should first find realistic answers to these assumptions and analyze them in detail. Of course, unless we want to deceive ourselves…

As we mentioned in various sections of this study; the success of the current program and the new three-year program which will be implemented from 2005, is dependent upon foreign finance support. For this reason, changing structural problems in the world, nonexistence of economic and political crises which can cause uncertainty, a competitive environment, a sustainable growth constitute the necessary prerequisites of the program…

However, if we analyze the current trend in the world economy, we can see that the basis of the assumption is shaky. The USA economy, as Sachs has stated in his article, is experiencing serious problems; a US $500 billion budget and US $500 billion foreign trade deficits are scary. On one side, the securities and real estates have been "overvalued" due to the low interest rates, and nobody wants to make sacrifices endangering his or her fortune. However, increasing raw material cost and particularly the oil prices constitute a serious threat to the developed countries. The costs bring an inflationist pressure. The American policy which is trying to keep the oil prices at US $28 level per barrel is obviously not working, at least for the time being. The developments in Iraq and Venezuela continue to threaten the American petroleum policy.

Under these circumstances, all the countries are turning to alternative energy resources which may eventually increase their costs, too.

In brief, the working order of the competition and market economy in the world is deteriorating. The developed countries are taking precautionary measures to prevent this, but the results are not successful up to now. The world economy in which the income distribution is not fair, is under the shadow of uncertainties. The US is trying to balance the twin deficits by increasing the interest rates, but on the other hand this bears the risk that the securities and the real estates may lose their value. Some are trying to sell these assets before panic prevails. In other countries such as the UK, there are some attempts to raise the interest rates…

Is it possible to get the necessary foreign funds for Turkey under the given circumstances? And even in the light of the fact that Turkey will be a net debt payer…

It seems impossible for the countries in need of foreign finance, to find borrowings in the international markets; and even if they can, the costs will be too high. The "mini crisis" which has been observed in April 2004 is the best example of this. In relation to the expectations of the increase in the USA interest rates and the resulting pressure it caused, the rates of the debt instruments of the countries like us rose from 7 percent to 9 percent and the trend turned upwards in the interest rates. Once again, it becomes obvious that it is not possible to attain a sustainable stability by making TL appreciate and achieving economic growth by increased domestic demand by means of reduced consumer credits which eventually create a foreign trade deficit. To find foreign finance will not be as easy as in the previous terms. Turkey which is the second most indebted country to the IMF, seems not to receive USA-backed IMF loans anymore. Nevertheless, the three-year IMF program which will be implemented from the beginning of 2005 can help delay the payments of the current debts, but the cost of this debt may also increase in parallel to the increasing interest rates in the world. As a result Turkey will bear a heavier interest burden.

On the other hand, increasing raw materials and oil prices will also affect the real sector. While the input costs are increasing, it will be inevitable for the public sector which holds the monopoly power, to reflect the increasing costs on the real sector and the consumers in order to prevent the tax losses. Even though it is contradictory to the inflation target, the public sector will continue to increase prices. Under these circumstances, the real sector will try to compensate these costs and lose its competitiveness.

While the real sector – which has difficulty in undertaking current costs and which, for this reason, abstains from creating additional employment – is increasing off-the-record, certain companies will have to leave their sectors. Exporters will attempt to obtain cheaper inputs in international markets instead of domestic producers because of the overvalued Turkish Lira, and thus they will try to keep some competitive power. Unemployment will continue. These negative developments in the real sector will naturally be reflected on the fiscal sector. Serious threats will appear in the restructuring process of the fiscal sector. The public sector's attempts to collect more taxes from the real sector may fail. This negative conjuncture will not attract the foreign investor to Turkey who cannot improve her investment environment and decrease input costs.

With current threats to the world economy, it seems not possible for Turkey to continue the current program supported by foreign finance in the forthcoming period. We have to admit that we cannot count on financing the foreign trade deficit by hot money under these negative conditions. A new economic program in line with the developments in the world economy must be immediately prepared and put into effect.

REFERENCES

BOOKS & ARTICLES

Bruno, M. *Crisis, Stabilisation and Economic Reform*, Oxford, Oxford University Press, 1993

Eğilmez, M. & Kumcu E. *Ekonomi Politikası*, Istanbul, OM Yayınevi, 2002

Eğilmez, M. & Kumcu, E. *Krizleri Nasıl Çıkardık*, Istanbul, Creative Yayıncılık, 2001

Erçel, G. "Disinflation Program for the Year 2000: Implementation of Exchange Rate and Monetary Policy", December 9, 1999, www.tcmb.gov.tr/yeni/eng/index.html

Fischer, S. "Exchange Rate Regimes: Is the Bipolar View Correct?", www.imf.org

Frankel, J. "Verifying Exchange Rate Regimes" with Eduardo Fajnzylber, Sergio Schmukler, and Luis Serven, *Journal of Development Economics*, vol. lxxi, no. 809, October 2001, pp. 351–386.

Frankel, J. "The New Financial Architecture: Exchange Rate Regimes and Financial Integration", Policy Brief no. 51, The Brookings Institution, Washington DC, June 1999

Karacan, A.İ. *Finans, Ekonomi ve Politika*, Istanbul, Creative Yayıncılık, 1997

Krugman, P. *Bunalım Ekonomisinin Geri Dönüşü*, Istanbul, Literatür, 2001

Nye, Joseph S. *Amerikan Gücünün Paradoksu*, Istanbul, Literatür Yayınları, 2003

Nye, Joseph S. *The Paradox of American Power*, Oxford, Oxford University Press, 2002

Parasız, İ. *Kriz Ekonomisi/Hiper Enflasyon ve Yüksek Enflasyonla Mücadelede Ünlü İstikrar Politikaları ve 5 Nisan 1994 Kararları*, Istanbul, Ezgi Yayınevi, 1996

Parasız İ. *Enflasyon-Kriz-Ayarlamalar/Dünyada ve Türkiye'de Kalkınma Makro Ekonomisi Sorunları*, Istanbul, Ezgi Yayınevi, 2001

Sachs, J.D. "Lessons from America's Fiscal Recklessness", December 2003, www.project-syndicate.org/commentaries/commentary-text.php

Sachs, J.D. "The Decline of America", March 2004, www.project-syndicate.org/commentaries/commentary-text.php

Stiglitz, J.E. *90'ların Yükselişi*, CSA Gobal Yayın Ajansı, 2003

Uygur, E. "Krizden Krize Türkiye: 2000 Kasım ve 2001 Şubat Krizleri", Türkiye Ekonomi Kurumu, Tartışma Metni No. 2001/1, Nisan, 2001

Uzunoğlu, S. "Ekonomiyi Önümüzdeki Dönemde Etkileyecek Olası Gelişmeler" *Mercek Dergisi*, Temmuz, 2004

REPORTS, JOURNALS AND OTHER DOCUMENTS

Stand-By Arrangement, Letter of Intent, Turkey, December 9, 1999, www.hazine.gov.tr

IMF Letter of Intent, December 18, 2000, www.hazine.gov.tr

IMF Letter of Intent, January 30, 2001, www.hazine.gov.tr

IMF Letter of Intent, June 26, 2001, www.hazine.gov.tr

New Stand-By Arrangement 2002–2004, Letter of Intent, January 18, 2002, www.hazine.gov.tr

Hazine Dergisi "Cumhuriyetin 80.Yılı Özel Sayısı"

İTKİB, *İhracat Performans Değerlendirmesi*, 2004

MÜSİAD, Araştırma Yayınları, "2004 Türkiye Ekonomisi", Mayıs 2004

T.C. Başbakanlık Hazine Müsteşarlığı, "Enflasyonla Mücadele Programı Politika Metinleri", Cilt 1, 2000

T.C. Başbakanlık Hazine Müsteşarlığı, "Enflasyonla Mücadele Programı Politika Metinleri", Cilt 2, 2001

WEBSITES

www. tcmb.gov.tr (Central Bank of the Republic of Turkey)

www.hazine.gov.tr (Turkish Treasury)

www.die.gov.tr (State Institute of Statistics)

www.tbb.org.tr (Bank Association of Turkey)

www.bddk.org.tr (Bank Regulation and Supervision Agency)

www.imf.org (International Monetary Fund)